DECODING THE STARS

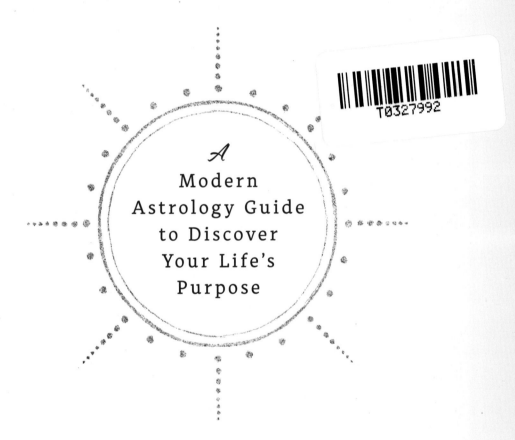

A
Modern
Astrology Guide
to Discover
Your Life's
Purpose

Allison Scott

WELLFLEET
PRESS

Inspiring | Educating | Creating | Entertaining

Brimming with creative inspiration, how-to projects, and useful information to enrich your everyday life, quarto.com is a favorite destination for those pursuing their interests and passions.

First published in 2023 by Wellfleet Press, an imprint of The Quarto Group,
142 West 36th Street, 4th Floor, New York, NY 10018, USA
T (212) 779-4972 F (212) 779-6058 www.Quarto.com

Wellfleet titles are also available at discount for retail, wholesale, promotional, and bulk purchase. For details, contact the Special Sales Manager by email at specialsales@quarto.com or by mail at The Quarto Group, Attn: Special Sales Manager, 100 Cummings Center Suite 265D, Beverly, MA 01915 USA.

10 9 8 7 6 5 4 3 2 1

ISBN: 978-1-57715-329-0

Library of Congress Cataloging-in-Publication Data

Names: Scott, Allison (Astrologer), author.
Title: Decoding the stars : a modern astrology guide to discover your
  life's purpose / Allison Scott.
Description: New York, NY : Wellfleet Press, 2023. | Series: Complete
  illustrated encyclopedia; 11 | Includes index. | Summary: "Decoding the
  Stars provides guidance for self-development and gives direction to
  those struggling with life's challenges by examining the details of your
  birth chart and, through guided rituals, giving fresh, new life to the
  practice of astrology"-- Provided by publisher.
Identifiers: LCCN 2022025466 (print) | LCCN 2022025467 (ebook) | ISBN
  9781577153290 (paperback) | ISBN 9780760377857 (ebook)
Subjects: LCSH: Astrology. | Birth charts.
Classification: LCC BF1708.1 .S38 2023 (print) | LCC BF1708.1 (ebook) |
  DDC 133.5--dc23/eng/20220715
LC record available at https://lccn.loc.gov/2022025466
LC ebook record available at https://lccn.loc.gov/2022025467

Group Publisher: Rage Kindelsperger
Creative Director: Laura Drew
Senior Managing Editor: Cara Donaldson
Editors: Katharine Moore and Elizabeth You
Cover and Interior Design: Laura Shaw Design

Printed in China

Contents

Introduction 6

Understanding the Code 12

PART I. YOUR CORE SELF 23
Chapter 1. Your Sun Sign: Your Essential Nature 24
Chapter 2. Your Sun House: Where You Are Energized 52
CRACKING THE CODE: YOUR CORE SELF 82

PART II. YOUR MOTIVATION 85
Chapter 3. Your Rising Sign: What Motivates You 86
Chapter 4. Your Rising Sign Ruler: Where You Are Steered 114
CRACKING THE CODE: YOUR MOTIVATION 132

PART III. YOUR EMOTIONAL WELL-BEING 135
Chapter 5. Your Moon Sign: Your Emotional Nature 136
Chapter 6. Your Moon House: Where You Find Emotional Fulfillment 164
CRACKING THE CODE: YOUR EMOTIONAL WELL-BEING 182

PART IV. YOUR WORK 185
Chapter 7. Your Houses of Substance 186
Chapter 8. Houses of Substance: Earth 192
Chapter 9. Houses of Substance: Air 199
Chapter 10. Houses of Substance: Water 206
Chapter 11. Houses of Substance: Fire 213
CRACKING THE CODE: YOUR WORK 220

Calibration 223

About the Author / Acknowledgments 233
References 234
Index 236

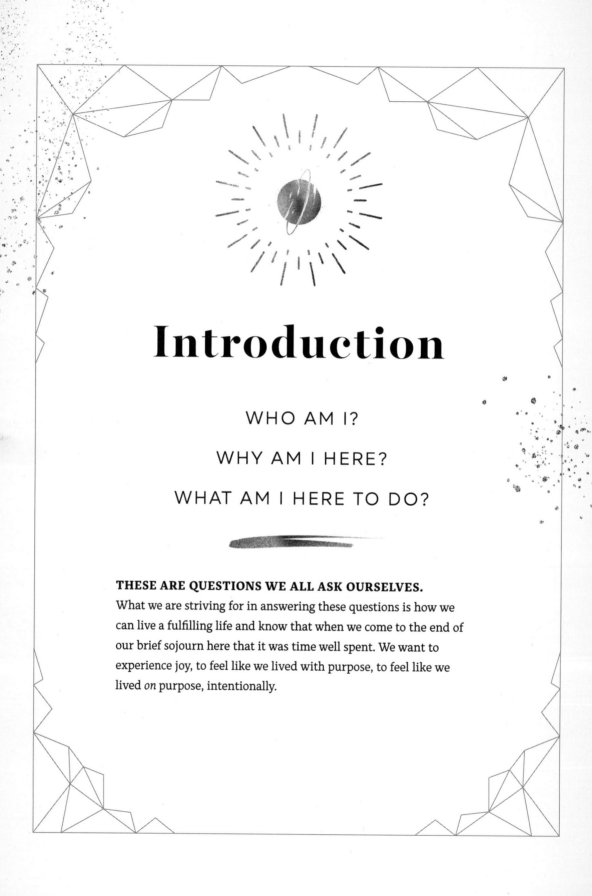

Introduction

WHO AM I?

WHY AM I HERE?

WHAT AM I HERE TO DO?

THESE ARE QUESTIONS WE ALL ASK OURSELVES.
What we are striving for in answering these questions is how we can live a fulfilling life and know that when we come to the end of our brief sojourn here that it was time well spent. We want to experience joy, to feel like we lived with purpose, to feel like we lived *on* purpose, intentionally.

There is a disconcerting, insidious inertia to life. Even though we make countless decisions daily and think, in our hectic scramble, that we are truly living, how many of us have stopped and realized years have passed in the same unfulfilling job, the same stifling town, the same misaligned mediocrity? In the horror of that moment, you may feel an itch to run, to burn it all down, to quit your job and move across the world—and perhaps that is your path. But living reactively can bring about its own set of problems. To live intentionally, we need a bit of patience, self-reflection, and wisdom.

Astrology provides us potent wisdom cultivated over thousands of years and gives us a means of structuring our introspection. Astrology has helped me live a more intentional, peaceful, joyful, fulfilling life. It has helped me counsel clients to do the same. And in this book, I'll help you understand how, by decoding the stars, you too can better understand yourself and your life's purpose.

You're Here for a Purpose

I used to think that finding my purpose was about identifying a task. What is it that I should be *doing*? How should I fill my time? What should I create? What activities will give my life meaning? I've come to understand that identifying our vocation is the result of understanding our own true nature: What are our core traits? What motivates us? What inspires us? What makes us feel safe? Once we understand our nature and choose to live authentically, we can then identify the activities that feel meaningful for us. Even more glorious, I've found that the more authentically and intentionally we live, the more serendipity and luck we experience. It is as though, by shedding all that is not us and enthusiastically claiming our true nature, we can begin to cocreate with the universe. It is then that we experience flow. It is then that our life is suffused with magic.

But how can we understand our true nature and live consciously and intentionally? This is where astrology comes in.

Astrology studies correlations between the movement of celestial objects (e.g., planets, luminaries, asteroids) and what transpires here on Earth. What happens in the heavens describes what is happening in our world. As above, so below. Our knowledge of this phenomenon has been accumulated over millennia. The Western tradition of astrology now practiced has roots stretching back 4,000 years to Mesopotamia, where astrologers carefully cataloged celestial omens and the terrestrial events they foretold. During the 5th century BCE, though, a new, more personal branch of astrology began to emerge. Astrologers started analyzing the placement of the Sun, Moon, and planets at the moment of a person's birth to divine information about their nature and fate. This practice, which we refer to as natal astrology, has developed over the last 2,500 years and still has valuable wisdom for us in our modern age.

The fundamental premise of natal astrology is that you were born to be you. The moment you first drew breath was not happenstance, but fated, and the placement of the stars and planets at

BEING IN FLOW

When our lives are in a state of flow, we perceive a sense of alignment. Our thoughts and actions feel right to us, and there is a sense of supportive response from the people and the world around us. Things feel as though they are falling into place and progressing. This doesn't mean that when we are in flow things are easy. You may be exerting a great amount of effort in activities that make you feel in flow. But there is a rightness and joy in this state that is enthralling. When we talk about finding our path and purpose, what we are seeking is this feeling of rightness. We cannot be in this state all the time, and which activities and choices feel in alignment will evolve as we grow and change. Through self-reflection and testing out choices intentionally, thoughtfully, and playfully, we can continue to recalibrate our lives to a flow state. Astrology aids in the self-reflection necessary for you to find the path that makes you feel in flow.

that moment gives insight to that fate. You were born on purpose. You were born *for* a purpose. By decoding your personal birth chart, you will come to better understand your nuanced, complex self and consciously claim all that is you. From this self-knowledge, you can then build an authentic life and experience the contentment and flow that such alignment offers. What work you do, what rest you enjoy, what relationships you forge, and what art you create become an expression of your true nature.

YOUR LIFE'S PURPOSE IS TO BE YOU.

Perhaps you're wondering, if you are destined to live out your natal astrology, then why look into it at all? Won't you just live out your fate? While the balance between free will and fate has been a heated debate among astrologers and philosophers throughout the ages, as a practicing astrologer, I've noticed two things that convince me of the value of astrology.

First, understanding your natal astrology helps you identify what is you and what is not you. Our society isn't built for self-actualization. Pervasive oppressions like systemic racism, misogyny, bigotry of every kind, capitalism, homogenizing education, and stifling religions and creeds push and pull us into a painful, monstrous shape. Astrology gives us a language and a methodology for interrogating which parts of our life and identity feel authentic to us and which are imposed upon us. Astrology helps us name and claim parts of ourselves that the dominant culture would rather we stifle. This is the work of a lifetime: to know and embrace who we are, and shed who we are not.

Second, while you are always living out your birth chart, you could be doing it *better*. You could be more in alignment. Part of accomplishing this is that shedding of what is not you and claiming what you've been forced to deny. But astrology also helps you understand why something feels in alignment and how to do more of that. Many of my clients are dissatisfied with their jobs, but that doesn't mean they are in the wrong career. There is a reason they are in that role and that field. It is an expression of their true nature. But what is it about that role that feels right and in flow? Whether you are a doctor or a hair stylist or a therapist, if you have water for your Houses of Substance (see part IV), then there is an inherent focus on relationships, intuition, and emotional connection in your work. Someone with the same profession but has earth for their Houses of Substance will feel engaged at work in a totally different way. Understanding key aspects of your chart will help you identify what about your work vibes with your nature, and what doesn't, so that you can try to increase what feels best and try and limit what feels stifling. We can't fully avoid tasks and situations we don't enjoy, but we can adjust the balance so that more of our time and energy is spent engaged in what makes us feel alive. This recalibration could require only minor changes, or it could lead you to make major shifts in your job or living situation.

I want to stress that you aren't doing anything wrong, wherever you are in your journey. You may feel lost, but you are already on the path. Everything you've experienced provides information to guide where you should go next. Everything that's happened—pain or joy, failure or success—has shaped you. Know, too, that being in alignment with your true nature and living out your purpose will not eliminate all suffering. Indeed, there might be *more* suffering by living your truth in a world that may not accept it. But there are gifts and joys to be had, too, when we renounce our lives of quiet desperation. My wish for you is that you feel fully alive and present in your life. That your life has meaning to you. That you choose to step into your wholeness with self-knowledge and intention and live on purpose every day of this precious life.

9

How to Use This Book

This book will take you step by step through decoding your birth chart to help you understand yourself and your life's purpose. Because most of us spend a lot of our time working, much of the focus of the book will be on what activities and work you're called to do. It's important to note, though, that a lot of the pleasure and fulfillment we get out of life is through activities we don't get paid for and meaningful relationships. When reading through the book and decoding your birth chart, consider how the descriptions apply in your personal and professional life. Also note that not every aspect of every placement will apply to you. This book is intended to be a self-reflection tool, not a rigid instruction manual. Ultimately, you know yourself best, so take what resonates and leave what doesn't.

In order to unlock the wisdom of astrology, you'll first need to learn the language, symbols, and metaphors of this ancient system. In **Understanding the Code**, you'll learn the basics of astrology, how to pull your birth chart, the different elements that make up a birth chart, and how to read it.

Once you're familiar with the language of astrology, you can then begin to decode your birth chart. Each chapter of the book will take you through a different facet of your chart. The chapters are intended to be read in order, with the most fundamental topics covered first; however, the chapters can stand alone and you may prefer to dip into whichever topic calls to you most.

The journey begins with **Part I: Your Core Self** and learning how your natal Sun placement explains your essential nature and where in life you feel most energized. Next, in **Part II: Your Motivation**, we'll consider how your Rising sign and its ruling planet or luminary describe what drives you and where your life is being steered. In **Part III: Your Emotional Well-being**, we'll discuss how your Moon sign and house explain how you feel emotionally safe, regulated, and fulfilled. These three aspects of your chart—your Sun, Rising, and Moon—provide the essential foundation for decoding your true nature and life's purpose.

Once you've gotten familiar with these essential aspects of self, we'll dig into what the birth chart has to say about your career. In **Part IV: Your Work**, we'll review how you manage your money and assets, the skills you use to earn money, how you prefer to structure your daily work, and the overarching style of your career and public life.

Each part concludes with **Cracking the Code**, a series of reflection questions that helps you unpack that aspect of your chart further, consider how it has influenced your life so far, and discern how you might apply the information to feel more in flow.

In the final section, **Calibration**, we'll walk through how to balance these different aspects of your chart. You'll consider how the qualities of your Sun, Rising, Moon, and Houses of Substance have shown up in your life, why certain parts of your chart resonate more than others, and how the elements support or challenge each other. We'll close where we began: by reflecting on your true nature, and how you can live authentically and purposefully.

May you see yourself more
clearly and more lovingly.

May you find what enlivens you and
grab hold of it with both hands.

May you live out the fullest
expression of your stars.

And so it is.

Understanding the Code

BEFORE DIVING INTO DECODING YOUR BIRTH CHART, you'll first need to familiarize yourself with the language and symbols of astrology. Astrology is a complex discipline, but for our purposes, we'll focus on a few essential elements that help us unpack your life's purpose. This section will explain:

➤ What a birth chart is and how to pull yours

➤ What the planets, luminaries, and points mean in astrology and how to identify them in your chart

➤ The meanings of the houses in astrology

➤ The signs of the zodiac in your chart

The Birth Chart

Your personal astrological code is expressed visually as your birth chart. A birth chart is a diagram of the sky at the moment you were born, noting the positions of the planets and luminaries (Sun and Moon). Charts may also include other celestial bodies (e.g., asteroids) as well as calculated points (e.g., the Midheaven).

The birth chart is drawn as a circle representing the ecliptic—that is, the apparent path the Sun, Moon, and planets traverse through the constellations of the zodiac throughout the year. The ecliptic (and therefore the birth chart) is broken into twelve equal sections of 30 degrees. Each 30-degree section corresponds to one of the twelve zodiacal signs. In a birth chart, each of the twelve signs resides in one of the twelve houses.

Placed around the birth chart are glyphs representing the various planets, luminaries, and points, which indicate where they were along the ecliptic at the moment you were born. See the Parts of the Birth Chart figure, noting the placement of the planets, the house numbers, and the zodiacal signs.

PARTS OF THE BIRTH CHART

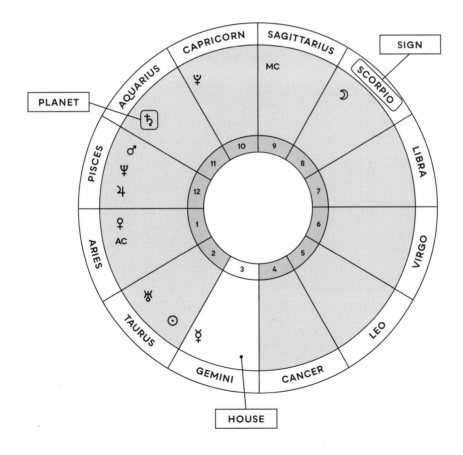

You may notice in the Parts of the Birth Chart figure that there is one zodiacal sign per house: Aries takes up the whole 1st House, Taurus the 2nd House, and so on. This kind of house drawing system is called Whole Sign Houses and has been around for some 2,000 years. Whole Sign Houses appears to have been the primary house system used in Hellenistic astrology—that is, the astrology developed by Greek-speaking astrologers in the 1st century BCE—which became the foundation for all Western astrology. In astrology's long history, many house drawing systems have been developed and astrologers use the one they find resonates with them and their clients best. My preference is to use Whole Sign Houses, but if you prefer another system (e.g., Placidus) the information in this book will still be valid for you. For example, the information about the house placement of your Moon by sign and house is relevant regardless of which house system you use.

Now that you have an idea of what a birth chart looks like, let's dig into the key parts:

➢ the Ascendant point and Rising sign

➢ the houses

➢ the zodiacal signs

➢ the planets, luminaries, and points

14

THE ASCENDANT POINT AND THE RISING SIGN

In order to draw your birth chart, you need to first determine the Ascendant point, which is the exact degree of the zodiac aligned to the eastern horizon at the moment of your birth. That Ascendant point will reside in a particular zodiacal sign. For example, author Ursula K. Le Guin was born when the eastern horizon was at 2 degrees of Taurus, so her Ascendant point is 2 degrees of Taurus. The Rising sign is the zodiacal sign containing the Ascendant point. So, Le Guin's Rising sign is Taurus.

In the Whole Sign Houses system, your Rising sign establishes the 1st House, and the 1st House contains the whole 30 degrees of the Rising sign. The 2nd House contains the entire 30 degrees of the next zodiacal sign—in Le Guin's case, Gemini. This continues, with each successive house containing the next whole sign in the order of the zodiac.

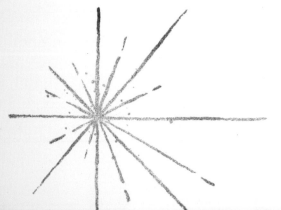

URSULA K. LE GUIN'S BIRTH CHART

BIRTH DATE: October 21, 1929
BIRTH TIME: 5:31 p.m.
BIRTH LOCATION: Berkeley, California

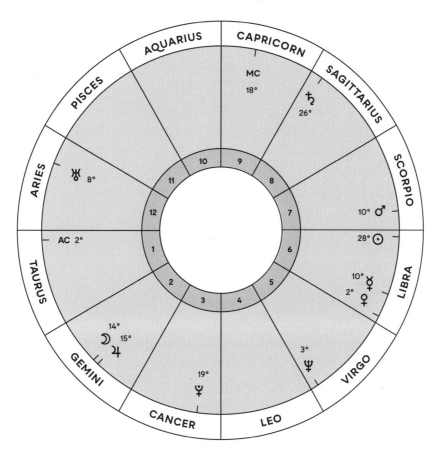

Because the Ascendant point and Rising sign establish the 1st House and therefore the whole chart setup, it is imperative to calculate the Ascendant point as accurately as possible. It takes about two hours for the Earth to rotate through 30 degrees of the ecliptic, so the Rising sign changes about every two hours. Depending on when you were born, even ten minutes could make the difference between having your Ascendant point in one sign or another, so the closer you can get to an exact birth time, the better. In some places, a person's birth time is listed on their birth certificate. Other times, you'll have to rely on family members, time-stamped photographs, or other records to establish your birth time. If you can't be sure about your birth time, you can work with an astrologer that specializes in rectification, the procedure by which astrologers correlate aspects of your life, personality, and major events to determine your probable birth time and Rising sign.

ASCENDANT POINT AND RISING SIGN

Your Rising sign is the zodiacal sign that was rising over the eastern horizon at the moment you were born (e.g., Taurus). At that moment, the horizon was aligned with a specific degree of your Rising sign (e.g., 3 degrees of Taurus), and that degree is known as your Ascendant point. The Rising sign is sometimes referred to as the Ascendant sign or simply the Ascendant, which can get a little confusing. For clarity, in this book, we'll only use the term *Ascendant point* to refer to the exact degree of your Rising sign aligned to the eastern horizon when you were born. When discussing the whole sign, we'll stick with calling it the Rising sign.

HOUSES

The birth chart is broken up into twelve segments, called houses. Each house signifies several topics of life (see the House Meanings chart). In the Whole Sign Houses system, the birth chart is divided into twelve equal-size houses and each house contains the whole 30 degrees of a single zodiacal sign. Multiply 30 degrees by the twelve houses and you get the full 360 degrees of a circle. The sign within the house provides information as to the nature and style of the aspects of life and personality signified by that house. For example, Le Guin's 6th House is occupied by Libra, so her day-to-day work, rituals, habits, and personal health would take on Libran qualities. Taken together, the houses provide a picture of your complete nature and how you relate to all aspects of life.

While all the houses, their signs, and the planets within those houses give information about you and your life, in this book we will focus on a few houses that give particularly useful insight into your life's purpose. We'll decode the meaning of your Sun house (chapter 2), your Rising sign's ruling planet's house (chapter 4), and your Moon house (chapter 6). We'll also consider your Houses of Substance (i.e., the 2nd, 6th, and 10th Houses, in part IV).

HOUSE MEANINGS

HOUSE	MEANING
1	Self and identity
2	Your money, assets, and the skills with which you make money
3	Communication, siblings, local neighborhood
4	Home, family, childhood home and family of origin, ancestors and lineage
5	Creativity, creative projects, and children
6	Day-to-day work, routines, habits, and personal health
7	Committed partnership (romantic, business, platonic)
8	Shared assets and resources, endings and transformations, grief and mental health
9	Learning, teaching, publishing; spiritual and philosophical beliefs, long-distance travel
10	Career and public life
11	Communities, friend groups, patrons and clients
12	Unconscious psychological material, connection to the collective unconscious and divine wisdom, secrets and hidden things

ZODIACAL SIGNS

We often think of our "sign" as our Sun sign (the zodiacal sign the Sun was in when you were born), but all birth charts contain all twelve zodiacal signs. We all contain every sign. Which house a sign occupies tells us about the nature of the life topics that correspond to that house. Considering, again, Ursula K. Le Guin's chart, knowing that Gemini is in her 2nd House gives us information about how she handles her money and the skills with which she makes money.

Signs also influence the expression of planets, luminaries, and points. For example, think of your Sun sign. The Sun in astrology represents our core self, what energizes us, and how we shine in the world. Do you feel that the traits of your Sun sign describe your core self (see chapter 1)? We'll dive deep into how various zodiacal signs show up in your chart throughout the book. For now, it's important to note that every sign has three key qualities:

➤ **ELEMENT** (earth, air, water, fire)

➤ **MODALITY** (cardinal, fixed, mutable)

➤ **PLANETARY RULER(S)**

The significance of a sign's element, modality, and planetary ruler will be unpacked throughout the book.

Note that some signs have two ruling planets: a traditional and a modern one. For the majority of astrology's long history, astrologers only worked with the visible planets (Mercury, Venus, Mars, Jupiter, and Saturn). As Uranus, Neptune, and Pluto were discovered, astrologers assigned them as modern rulers of the zodiacal signs Aquarius, Pisces, and Scorpio, respectively. Both rulers have their place in interpreting the birth chart. When it is important to consider one ruler instead of another (specifically in chapter 4, Your Rising Sign Ruler), we'll dig into the reasoning behind that choice.

SIGN	SYMBOL	MODALITY	ELEMENT	RULERS
Aries	♈	Cardinal	Fire	Mars
Taurus	♉	Fixed	Earth	Venus
Gemini	♊	Mutable	Air	Mercury
Cancer	♋	Cardinal	Water	Moon
Leo	♌	Fixed	Fire	Sun
Virgo	♍	Mutable	Earth	Mercury
Libra	♎	Cardinal	Air	Venus
Scorpio	♏	Fixed	Water	Mars and Pluto
Sagittarius	♐	Mutable	Fire	Jupiter
Capricorn	♑	Cardinal	Earth	Saturn
Aquarius	♒	Fixed	Air	Saturn and Uranus
Pisces	♓	Mutable	Water	Jupiter and Neptune

LUMINARIES, PLANETS, AND POINTS

The last components of the birth chart we'll consider are:

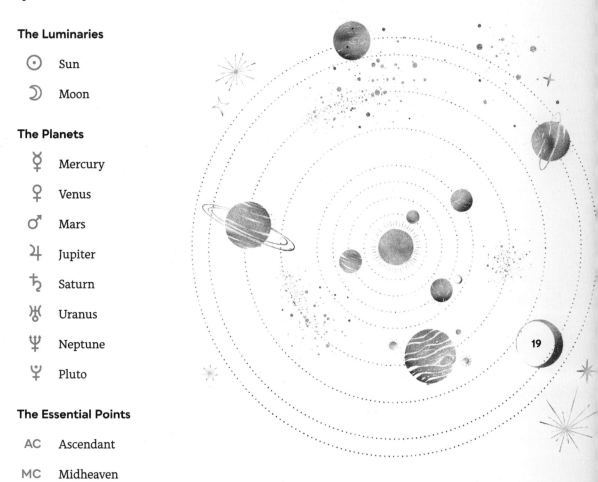

The Luminaries

☉   Sun

☽   Moon

The Planets

☿   Mercury

♀   Venus

♂   Mars

♃   Jupiter

♄   Saturn

♅   Uranus

♆   Neptune

♇   Pluto

The Essential Points

AC   Ascendant

MC   Midheaven

Each luminary, planet, and point speaks to different aspects of your personality. For example, the Sun represents your core self and the Moon represents your emotional nature and needs. Their placement by sign and house gives us information as to your nature. The Midheaven, or Medium Coeli (MC), is a calculated point that represents the highest point the Sun reached along the ecliptic on the day of your birth. The Midheaven provides information about your public life, career path, and reputation.

In this book, we'll be focusing on significations of the Sun (part I), Rising Sign and its ruler (part II), Moon (part III), and Midheaven (part IV), because these components provide the most essential information in decoding your life's purpose.

A NOTE ABOUT SCOPE

Astrology is a complex discipline too expansive to be discussed in any one book. This book omits some important astrological considerations, like planetary aspects and condition. The components of your birth chart discussed in this book will give you a great deal of information about your nature, life's purpose, and the work you're here to do in the world. The goal of this book is to help you understand your nature so you can work with your innate qualities and tendencies to feel more in flow, feel more fulfilled, and live more intentionally. Further research and getting a consultation from an astrologer can help you go deeper into the nuances of your chart.

How to Pull Your Chart

In order for you to make use of this book, you will need to acquire a copy of your birth chart. There are many websites that allow you to download your birth chart for free. I recommend Cafe Astrology, which is a great resource for free astrological information. You can pull your birth chart drawn according to Whole Sign Houses here:

https://cafeastrology.com/free-natal-chart-report-whole-sign-houses.html

Astro.com is another great free resource for pulling your birth chart.

All you need to calculate your birth chart is your birth date, time, and location. Remember, getting as accurate a birth time as possible is essential.

Decoding Your Stars

Once you have your birth chart in hand, complete the **My Astro Code** summary. You can then approach the book by reading the entry for each of your placements in order, or by reading the parts that call to you most. At the end of each part is a section called **Cracking the Code**, which will walk you through how to unpack what you've learned in the preceding chapters. After reading parts I through IV, check out the final section, **Calibration**, to understand how you can put all you've learned together into a cohesive story about you and your life's purpose.

MY ASTRO CODE

My Sun sign is _____.

My Sun is in the _____House.

My Moon sign is _____.

My Moon is in the _____House.

My Rising sign is _____.

My Rising sign ruler is _____.

My Rising sign ruler is in the _____House.

My 2nd House sign is _____.

My 6th House sign is _____.

My 10th House sign is _____.

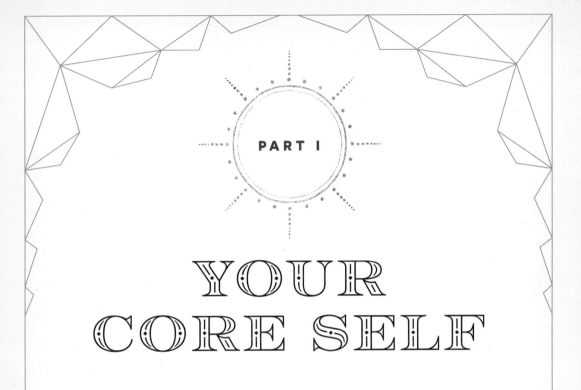

PART I

YOUR CORE SELF

THE SUN IS THE CENTER OF OUR SOLAR SYSTEM. Everything revolves around it, pulled by its undeniable gravitational force. It is what we use to measure our lives—in days and nights, and in years as the Earth makes its annual trek around it. The Sun's energy warms us, causes plants to grow, and enables life to flourish. Likewise, the Sun in your birth chart is your vitality, your engine, your center, and your very core essence.

There are two primary considerations when interpreting your Sun placement: **sign** and **house**. The zodiacal sign the Sun was in when you were born describes your core nature, which you are compelled to express in the world. It is your vibe and your essential way of being. Your Sun house describes where in life you shine and feel most energized. It gives insight into what activities are most important to you, come most naturally, and make you feel most in flow.

Your life's purpose is to embody the fullest, most authentic expression of your true self—as described by the entirety of your birth chart—so understanding your core nature through interpreting the Sun's placement in your chart is the foundation of decoding your purpose.

1

Your Sun Sign

YOUR ESSENTIAL NATURE

IF YOU KNOW just one thing about your natal astrology, it is most likely your Sun sign. The Sun spends about thirty days in each sign, and since the advent of popular Sun sign horoscopes in newspapers and magazines in the early 20th century, it's become nearly ubiquitous that a person knows the sign the Sun was in when they were born. Sun signs are often reduced to simplistic lists of personality traits—Aries is always angry, Libra is always flirting, Pisces is always crying, Taurus is always napping. These kinds of lists make for great memes, but most often people feel alienated by reductive traits that don't describe them or that often cast them in a negative light. We need a more nuanced understanding of the Sun sign in order to decode what it can tell us about our life's purpose.

The sign that your natal Sun is in describes your essential nature, the manner in which you want to shine in the world, and which activities energize you. Before learning more about your specific Sun sign, it is important to consider how the signs are grouped by two key properties: element and modality.

The **element** of your Sun sign describes whether your nature is focused on:

▽ **EARTH**   practical and material endeavors

△ **AIR**   communication and intellectual pursuits

▽ **WATER**   emotional intelligence, intuition, and relationships

△ **FIRE**   action and passion

The **modality** of your Sun sign speaks to your tendency to:

CARDINAL   initiate actions and lead

FIXED   stabilize situations and persist

MUTABLE   serve as an agent of change

Understanding the element and modality of your sign helps you realize the unique gifts and potential challenges you bring to the world, in all aspects of your life and work. Are you someone gifted at starting action (cardinal sign), or do you find it takes a lot of energy to get going (fixed)? On the flip side, do you have difficulty completing tasks (air and fire signs), or do you generally have the ability to see things through once you get started (earth)? As you read through your Sun sign's description, consider how the element and modality influence how your sign is expressed.

When thinking about your Sun sign and your life's purpose, consider when and how you've been able to express your essential nature. Which relationships, activities, and jobs allow you to express the nature of your Sun sign, and which stifle it? Try to recall a few instances in your personal and professional life where you fully embodied your nature. Did you feel energized? Did you feel in flow? You have many excellent and interesting qualities, but what your Sun sign helps you understand is what is core to you. What cannot and should not be denied. When evaluating whether a personal or professional opportunity aligns with your life's purpose, consider whether it taps into the vitality of your Sun sign essence and your preferred way of shining in the world. Trying to do more of what lights you up and less of what drains you will help guide your life into flow.

Depending on the balance of your chart (e.g., your Sun in a water sign, but most other planets and points are fire and air signs), or the kinds of social norms you're required to conform to, you may feel like your Sun sign qualities aren't dominant. See the concluding section, **Calibration**, for more information on balancing the various elements of your chart. Reflecting on how the qualities of your Sun sign show up in your life may uncover latent skills, preferences, and drives that have been sidelined by other qualities that you've been required or encouraged to prioritize. How can you reclaim these aspects of self?

Remember that this is just the first step in decoding your birth chart, so if you feel like only a portion of your Sun sign's description applies to you, that's good. There's a lot more to you than this one aspect!

YOUR SUN SIGN

Fill in the blanks with information from your own birth chart.

Your Sun sign: _____

Your Sun sign element: _____

Your Sun sign modality: _____

SUN IN ARIES

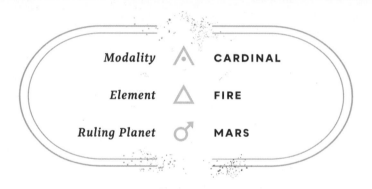

Modality	△	CARDINAL
Element	△	FIRE
Ruling Planet	♂	MARS

Courageous, passionate, and aggressive, **ARIES** is a sign of forward momentum and action. Its symbols are the sword, spear, and shield. Aries can be cutting, slicing through to the heart of the matter. Aries rends, separating what is worthy and discarding what must go. Aries destroys, toppling antiquated and unjust systems. Aries protects, shielding those in need and advocating for those who need their cause championed. A common perception of this sign is of its negative expression: hotheaded, brash, self-focused, cutting. In its positive, mature expression, Aries channels its extraordinary energy, resolve, and courage in service of a meaningful goal or ideal.

With your Sun in Aries, you may identify with the warrior archetype, finding fulfillment when fighting for a cause and drawn to the role of advocate. Sometimes, this innate need to champion a cause can be fulfilled in the workplace as a lawyer, social justice advocate, talent agent, or military servicemember. The primary job role doesn't have to be advocacy to be fulfilling, though, as long as your Aries Sun has an outlet for its righteous fervor, like defending the viability of a new project to the board or advocating for better workplace conditions. This warrior quality can also find expression in an Aries Sun's personal life, fighting for educational resources for their child or providing friends with aggressive pep talks. The passion, energy, courage, and tenacity of an Aries Sun needs to find expression for you to feel fulfilled.

Aries is also a sign of independence and individuality. On the other hand, as astrologer Christopher Renstrom points out in his book *The Cosmic Calendar*, Aries can be content serving under a worthy general to a noble end. This, however, isn't the easiest situation to be in. You may find satisfaction only in leadership roles, entrepreneurship, or work situations that limit bureaucracy and red tape. Primarily, you are happy when you are able to just get down to business and anything inhibiting your freedom to act will be frustrating.

Consider the house in which your Sun resides to see where in life you express your Aries energy to initiate action or be a warrior.

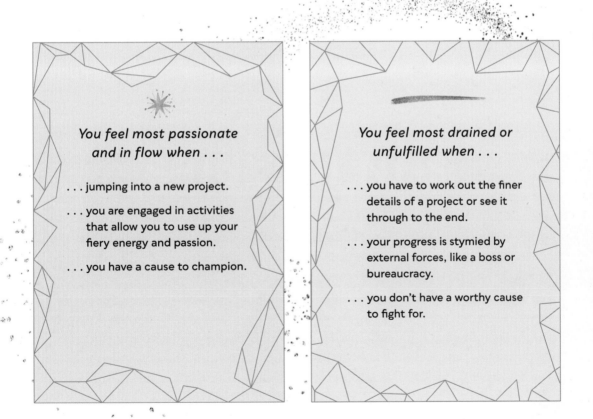

You feel most passionate and in flow when . . .

. . . jumping into a new project.

. . . you are engaged in activities that allow you to use up your fiery energy and passion.

. . . you have a cause to champion.

You feel most drained or unfulfilled when . . .

. . . you have to work out the finer details of a project or see it through to the end.

. . . your progress is stymied by external forces, like a boss or bureaucracy.

. . . you don't have a worthy cause to fight for.

SUN IN TAURUS

Modality	⊟	**FIXED**
Element	▽	**EARTH**
Ruling Planet	♀	**VENUS**

30

TAURUS is symbolized by the bull and is perhaps best known for its legendary stubbornness. This stubbornness, though, is but one manifestation of the core qualities of this fixed earth sign. As a fixed sign, Taurus stabilizes. It is inertia personified. Once settled on a course of action or a belief, it can take a Herculean effort to shift the bull to change course. How this positively manifests is through an extraordinary stamina to build things that take time. It may take a while to get started, but once set into motion, Taurus will drive forward with a steady consistency. Expressed negatively, a Taurus can tend to stay committed to projects that should be abandoned.

As an earth sign, Taurus's purpose in life is concerned with the material, physical world. Like a farmer, Taurus tills and prepares the ground, sows the seeds, and tends its crop, knowing that immense time and effort must be expended in order to reap the harvest. This is why Taurus can sometimes appear lazy or inactive to others (looking at you, fire signs). Taurus won't be rushed. Sometimes the fields should be left fallow to rest. Sometimes the majority of growth happens underground. Taurus doesn't need to make a show of their process for applause. Taurus knows what they are about and just gets on with it.

As a Venus-ruled sign, Taurus's purpose is deeply entwined with pleasure and beauty. Taureans unapologetically relish the pleasures of all five senses—good food and drink, fine music, engaging company, luxurious fabrics, heady scents. Where other signs might be stuck in their heads (air signs), focused on activity (fire signs), or engaged in emotional connection (water signs), Taurus reminds us to value our embodied existence as humans. Taurus's purpose marries Venusian pleasure with earth sign materialism. This can show up quite literally, working as a gardener, florist, visual artist, or craftsperson. The Venusian aspects of the Taurus's core self are expressed in whatever they do, though, not just their profession.

Consider the house in which your Sun resides to see where in life you express your Taurus energy in order to build, stabilize, beautify, and/or prioritize pleasure.

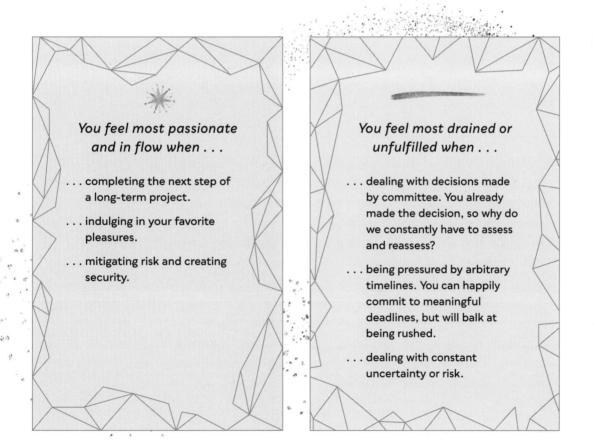

You feel most passionate and in flow when . . .

. . . completing the next step of a long-term project.

. . . indulging in your favorite pleasures.

. . . mitigating risk and creating security.

You feel most drained or unfulfilled when . . .

. . . dealing with decisions made by committee. You already made the decision, so why do we constantly have to assess and reassess?

. . . being pressured by arbitrary timelines. You can happily commit to meaningful deadlines, but will balk at being rushed.

. . . dealing with constant uncertainty or risk.

SUN IN GEMINI

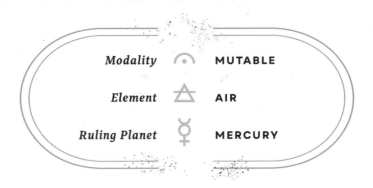

Modality		MUTABLE
Element		AIR
Ruling Planet		MERCURY

The symbol of **GEMINI** is the twins, illustrating the duality of Gemini and their unique ability to hold two divergent ideas at once, without judgment. Gemini isn't limited to either/or; they are masters of both/and. This Mercury-ruled sign's greatest gift is its insatiable curiosity, breadth of knowledge, and ability to hold and synthesize a multiplicity of ideas. Gemini Sun's life must honor their curious mind and the winding highways and byways it pulls them down.

I've spoken with many Gemini Suns who berate themselves for having too many interests, thinking that instead they should just focus on one passion. This is not an authentic expression of the Gemini Sun, however. It is the indoctrination of a culture that values specialization rather than generalization. In his book *Creativity: The Psychology of Discovery and Invention,* Mihaly Csikszentmihalyi laments that the tendency of our society to favor specialization stymies innovation, because the creativity that makes the greatest contribution most often involves the synthesis of multiple domains of knowledge.

To fully express your authentic self and align with your life's purpose, Gemini Suns must learn to see their voracious thirst for knowledge and novelty as a superpower, not an impediment. You are the unique lens through which this diversity of ideas is processed. What you can imagine is unique to you and the gift you give to the world.

Unless you have planets placed in earth signs, a challenge for Gemini Sun can be follow-through. It is a true expression of Gemini Sun to learn for the sake of learning, moving from one obsession to the next. Seeking careers that allow you to follow your curiosity will feel most supportive and fulfilling. Jobs that provide some external structures for organizing your thinking or committing to deadlines can be immensely helpful. This structure may feel like it stifles your creativity, but it's essential to find the right balance between the freedom to explore and the necessary accountability to bring projects to fruition. Interdisciplinary studies, melding different artistic mediums and modalities, cobbling together a career of different hustles, writing books on interdisciplinary topics, taking two seemingly divergent careers and seeing how they can be blended to create something new—these are the playground of the Gemini.

Consider the house in which your Sun resides to see where in life you focus your curiosity.

You feel most passionate and in flow when . . .

. . . researching your new favorite topic or learning a new skill.

. . . discussing ideas with others to generate new ideas or solutions.

. . . blending diverse ideas together to make new knowledge.

You feel most drained or unfulfilled when . . .

. . . repeating the same kinds of tasks or projects without an end or change in sight.

. . . confined to a rigid schedule or structure.

. . . working in isolation without the opportunity to exchange ideas and develop new ideas with other people.

SUN IN CANCER

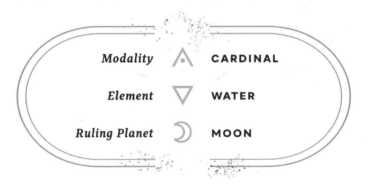

Modality	△	CARDINAL
Element	▽	WATER
Ruling Planet	☽	MOON

CANCER, as the cardinal water sign, is driven to initiate and cultivate relationships and social groups. Whether it's your friends, family, or work colleagues, you seek to create a community of people. People likely feel your inviting nature, even if you see yourself as having a prickly or hard exterior. People seek you out and tell you their secrets; perhaps you feel familiar to them, like home.

Cancers feel most fulfilled and in flow when they are able to use their gifts for compassion and caretaking. You are adept at truly listening to others and understanding their needs, even those they struggle to express. Cancers can find fulfillment in helping and healing professions, certainly, but any work with people—one-on-one with clients or in groups—where you can feel and cultivate a sense of belonging will be most fulfilling. Cutthroat environments and those that don't seek to cultivate their employees are anathema to you. Cancers know it takes a village and are determined to create that village.

Cancers often get a bad rap for being emotional and changeable—they are ruled by the ever-shifting Moon, after all. But even if the Crab has a soft center and a deep capacity for emotion, they also have a hard shell, which can manifest as impressive tenacity, resilience, and fortitude. You are strong, but you are not cold and unmovable. You have the strength to weather adversity and help others do so as well.

When thinking about your life's purpose, consider what the concepts of home and family mean to you. How do you cultivate a family at work, with relatives, and with friends? Are these relationships fulfilling to you? Specifically at work, when have you felt most supported, valued, and in flow? How important are the relationships at work to your sense of workplace satisfaction? Cancer Sun folks need to create that sense of familial camaraderie and duty at work in order to feel energized and like the work is meaningful. Whether running a small business where your employees are treated as family or being part of a tight-knit department in a large corporation, it is the quality of the relationships that will most impact your sense of satisfaction.

Consider the house in which your Sun resides to determine the areas of life where you are called to build a sense of home and to serve as the connector or caretaker.

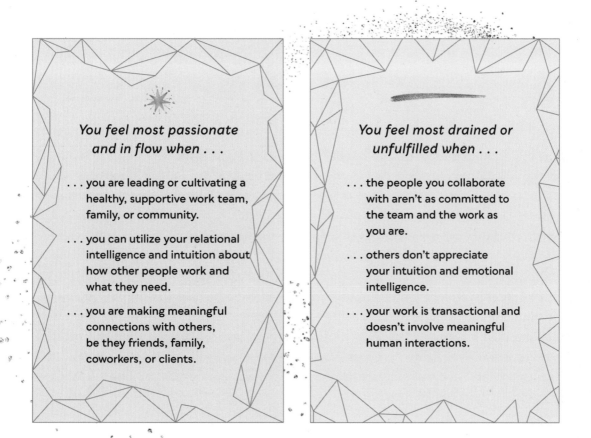

You feel most passionate and in flow when . . .

. . . you are leading or cultivating a healthy, supportive work team, family, or community.

. . . you can utilize your relational intelligence and intuition about how other people work and what they need.

. . . you are making meaningful connections with others, be they friends, family, coworkers, or clients.

You feel most drained or unfulfilled when . . .

. . . the people you collaborate with aren't as committed to the team and the work as you are.

. . . others don't appreciate your intuition and emotional intelligence.

. . . your work is transactional and doesn't involve meaningful human interactions.

SUN IN LEO

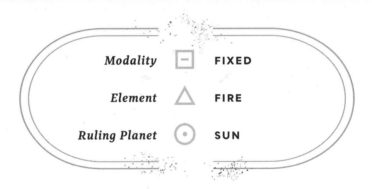

Modality	⊟	FIXED
Element	△	FIRE
Ruling Planet	⊙	SUN

The sign of **LEO** is ruled by the Sun, and like the Sun, the purpose of Leo is to shine. The Sun's energy is a vital contribution to the ecosystem. It enables growth, warmth, and illumination. Likewise, when a Leo shines their light, it is a contribution to the collective. The most important part of a Leo Sun's purpose is to express themselves authentically, whatever that means for them, and be recognized and appreciated for their performance. Determining who you are is the work of a lifetime, as you parse out what is truly you and what parts have been forced upon you. But sharing the messy truth of this self-exploration is authentic and valuable, too.

Leos are often described as wanting to be on stage, but what that means is that Leo is driven to be witnessed, acknowledged, and admired for their talents and performance—for their whole self. This core drive is negatively cast as egocentric, but all of us deserve to be seen, loved, understood, and applauded. We all have a Sun in our charts that wants to shine. By boldly taking up space and owning that they have something valuable to share, Leo teaches the rest of the zodiac that they, too, are worthy of acknowledgment and recognition.

Leo Sun folks, in their drive to shine their excellence, can also serve as an exemplar of human ability. In 2019, Leo Sun Nirmal Purja, along with his team of Nepali mountaineers, summited all fourteen of the world's 8,000-meter peaks (including Everest and K2) in only seven months, breaking numerous mountaineering records. In the film *14 Peaks: Nothing Is Impossible*, which documents his journey, Purja claims that one of his key motivations is to show what people are capable of. He wanted to inspire the human race. In its highest expression, Leo's superpower is the ability to awe and inspire.

Whether it's in front of a classroom, boardroom, live studio audience, podcast mic, or community group, Leo is ready and willing to step into the spotlight. To step forward, take up space, and share their passion. What stages call to you? In what areas of your life have you felt most seen, valued, and admired? What performances matter to you? What warmth do you want to share with others? What generosity? How do you want to inspire others?

Consider the house in which your Sun resides to get a better sense of where in life you want to shine and seek acknowledgment and admiration.

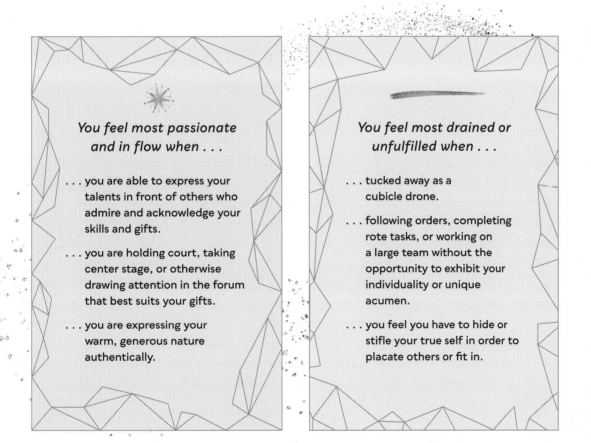

You feel most passionate and in flow when . . .

. . . you are able to express your talents in front of others who admire and acknowledge your skills and gifts.

. . . you are holding court, taking center stage, or otherwise drawing attention in the forum that best suits your gifts.

. . . you are expressing your warm, generous nature authentically.

You feel most drained or unfulfilled when . . .

. . . tucked away as a cubicle drone.

. . . following orders, completing rote tasks, or working on a large team without the opportunity to exhibit your individuality or unique acumen.

. . . you feel you have to hide or stifle your true self in order to placate others or fit in.

SUN IN VIRGO

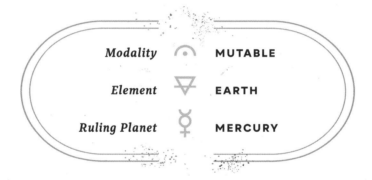

Modality	☉	**MUTABLE**
Element	▽	**EARTH**
Ruling Planet	☿	**MERCURY**

VIRGO is the earth sign ruled by Mercury, the planet of mental acuity, communication, and speed. A Virgo's swift mind is constantly working, solving problems and seeking to perfect. It's important for Virgos to have meaningful problems to solve, processes to improve, or products to refine, otherwise their busy mind can turn to self-criticism, anxiety, or excessive (and unwelcome) critique of others.

As an earth sign, Virgo is interested in practical, measurable solutions and clearly defined success criteria. Virgo isn't interested in admiring a problem or philosophizing. There is work to be done, and a Virgo will create a spreadsheet and checklist to ensure that everything is completed correctly and on time. Amorphous end goals are particularly frustrating to Virgos. How can we build a plan if we don't know where we are going or what success looks like? Professions where the job role is clearly defined, the goals are measurable and specific, and accountability is built in can be comforting and rewarding for Virgos (unless they have several planets in more freewheeling signs like Pisces, Sagittarius, and Gemini).

Though earth signs can often be intractable, Virgo is a mutable sign and as such is interested in change, specifically change that improves or perfects. It is difficult for a Virgo to be satisfied because their keen mind can always see room for improvement. This is the defining characteristic of a Virgo: discernment. A Virgo is uniquely capable of viewing the totality of a situation and discerning what needs to be cut or what needs to be improved.

Another key attribute of Virgo is service to others, especially in the medical profession or other healing modalities. Virgo's practicality and analytical mind feel most useful when applied in service to others. Virgo wants to be busy, but abhors busywork. Work with a purpose is most fulfilling, and the most purposeful work for a Virgo tangibly improves the lives of others.

When thinking of your life's purpose, when have you felt most energized employing your Virgoan gifts? What projects utilized your discernment and organizational skills? What activities keep your busy mind engaged? Has helping others been a central driving force in your life? In what ways would you like to employ your talents in service of others?

Consider the house in which your Sun resides to understand what areas of life you're most called to turn your Virgoan laser vision on to problem solve and perfect.

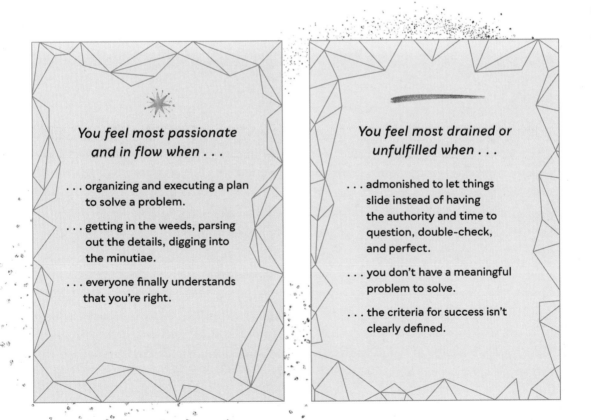

You feel most passionate and in flow when . . .

. . . organizing and executing a plan to solve a problem.

. . . getting in the weeds, parsing out the details, digging into the minutiae.

. . . everyone finally understands that you're right.

You feel most drained or unfulfilled when . . .

. . . admonished to let things slide instead of having the authority and time to question, double-check, and perfect.

. . . you don't have a meaningful problem to solve.

. . . the criteria for success isn't clearly defined.

SUN IN LIBRA

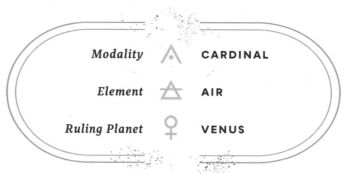

Modality	△	CARDINAL
Element	△	AIR
Ruling Planet	♀	VENUS

LIBRA is ruled by Venus, the goddess of beauty, relationships, connection, art, and pleasure. The core energy of Libra is harmony—bringing disparate elements together in pleasing balance. This drive to create balance can be fulfilled through any number of interests. A Libran artist, interior designer, or gallery curator is driven by the pleasure and power of aesthetic beauty. Libras take on roles like lawyer, mediator, or social worker to achieve justice, which idealistically creates order, balance, and fairness. While any sign might choose these professions, a Libra finds fulfillment in the creation of harmony from discord.

The desire for balance and harmony can mean that a Libra has little stamina when it comes to conflict. Even though Libras are adept at understanding multiple sides of an argument and negotiating compromises, they develop this skill set in part because they abhor disharmony and find it taxing. Libras who choose career paths that position them as peacemakers (diplomacy, law, counseling) need to counterbalance that work with home lives, relationships, and hobbies that provide them the peaceful respite they need to avoid burnout.

Libra is also the sign aligned with partnership and marriage. While Libras are often associated with the archetype of the socialite, it is in one-on-one relationships that Libras have unique power. Libras are gifted thought partners, confidants, coaches, and cheerleaders. Libras also greatly benefit from having partners to bounce ideas off of and to work with toward a common goal. Libras aren't keen to work in isolation. There is something magical that happens when they work with others that can't be achieved alone. Reflect on how you felt and what you accomplished when working with a partner. Was it fulfilling? Were those times of ingenuity and accomplishment? This isn't to say that Libras don't work well on teams—they generally get along with everyone—but you may find your most generative collaborations are with a single partner or small group.

When considering your life's purpose, in what ways do you strive for balance in your life and work? What talents do you have for cultivating harmony and which are most meaningful and enjoyable to you? Is aesthetic beauty a priority for you? What talents do you have for creating and sharing beauty? Is justice and peace your preferred domain of balance, and if so, through what means do you seek to facilitate justice? You will likely engage with all forms of balance—interpersonal harmony, justice, and aesthetic beauty—though you may find more flow in dedicating the majority of your time and energy to just one.

Consider the house in which your Sun resides to see where in life you want to bring balance and harmony, especially in partnership with others.

You feel most passionate and in flow when . . .

. . . collaborating in partnership with others.

. . . creating beauty, harmony, and peace in whatever way feels most meaningful to you.

. . . mediating people toward a just resolution.

You feel most drained or unfulfilled when . . .

. . . mired in unresolved conflict.

. . . working in isolation.

. . . subjected to crassness or rudeness.

SUN IN SCORPIO

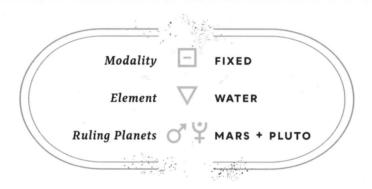

Modality	⊟	FIXED
Element	▽	WATER
Ruling Planets	♂ ♇	MARS + PLUTO

What is the truth? What really matters? Where are the bodies buried? These are the questions that drive **SCORPIO**. Ruled by Mars, Scorpio points its spear of incisive inquiry at its target and goes for blood. Scorpio doesn't have time for superficiality when the raw beauty and horror of reality is pushing in from all sides.

The gift of Scorpio to the collective is that they keep it real—uncomfortably so, for most people. Shocking people is a special skill—and pleasure—for this fixed water sign, and it's something humanity desperately needs. In a world of violence, cruelty, pain, addiction, loss, heartache, and suffering, most people would rather seek distraction, but Scorpio has the power to force us to see the shadow side we pretend isn't there. That which is ignored, taboo, or pushed to the periphery is the purview of Scorpio.

It's not all shock and awe, however. Like its modern ruler Pluto, god of the Underworld, Scorpio's great power is its understanding and facilitation of death, transformation, and rebirth. In recognizing horrific truth, we become able to address it and transmute it. Astrologer Chani Nicholas describes Scorpio's transformational power as the ability to collect the detritus of our lives,

42

compost it, and create fertile soil from which new life can grow. Whether through art, psychology, spirituality, or mergers and acquisitions, Scorpio is in alignment as a death doula, guiding the process of endings, transformation, and new beginnings.

Even though superficiality is tedious for Scorpio, it is a sign that excels at secrets and subterfuge, if they so choose. While bureaucratic maneuvering seems antithetical to Scorpio's desire for authenticity and brutal honesty, Scorpios can have a thirst for power, like Pluto, and may relish playing the corporate game to work their way up the ladder.

Scorpio's crusade for truth is often externally focused, as they reserve personal intimacy and self-disclosure for only a trusted few. It is only those rare individuals who are admitted to the inner sanctum of Scorpio's trust who experience the full depth and intensity of Scorpio's emotional range.

In what ways do you engage with difficult truths and taboo material? In what ways do you engage others in meaningful, difficult conversations and revelations? How do you facilitate transformation? What truths do you uncover?

Consider the house in which your Sun resides to see where in life you want to facilitate transformation, seek power, or excavate for the truth.

You feel most passionate and in flow when . . .

. . . engaging in matters of substance, especially topics that society shies away from and deems taboo.

. . . initiating and facilitating transformation for self or others.

. . . you have the power to influence others and effect change.

You feel most drained or unfulfilled when . . .

. . . performing social niceties or other superficial activities.

. . . your creative or professional work feels shallow and frivolous.

. . . subjected to a power imbalance at work where you have little control over what work is completed and how.

SUN IN SAGITTARIUS

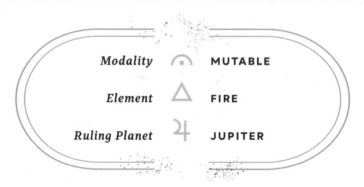

Modality	☉	**MUTABLE**
Element	△	**FIRE**
Ruling Planet	♃	**JUPITER**

SAGITTARIANS are perhaps best known for their adventurous spirit. Being a fire sign, Sagittarians are driven to act and have immense stores of energy. A mutable sign, Sagittarius revels in a diversity of experiences and can quickly become bored. The defining energy of Sagittarius is to seek—new ideas, new people, and new locations are always calling to the wandering Sagittarian spirit. But what are they seeking in each new adventure? Sagittarians are driven by a yearning to understand the big, philosophical, spiritual truths of life. Why are we here? What is reality? What is the nature of the Divine? What is the meaning of life? At the heart of their journeying, Sagittarians feel an insatiable yearning to understand.

Like other mutable signs, Sagittarians are most happy when their lives offer them enough variability and novelty. For some, their careers have enough built-in flexibility and changeability to keep them on their toes. For others, having a career that provides enough financial resources and vacation time for extended weekend getaways and larger, long-distance adventures will scratch that itch. Still others find the path of seeking leads them to the library, lecture hall, monastery, or temple. There is something of a philosophizing itinerant monk about every Sagittarian.

The daredevil spirit of Sagittarius doesn't seek out exhilarating experiences for the sole purpose of an adrenaline rush (although they often enjoy that, too). Sagittarians understand that the wisdom they seek cannot be found only in books, but rather must be invoked through experience. It isn't enough to be told the truth. Sagittarius has to feel it, see it, perceive it directly. Language is inadequate to communicate the ineffable, whereas experience can offer glimpses of transcendence.

When thinking about your life's purpose, consider what adventures, philosophy, or learning has been most exhilarating and engrossing for you. What are the big questions that call to you? What adventures make you feel most alive? What experiences feed your enthusiasm? How can you dedicate more time and resources to your preferred exploits?

**Consider the house in which your Sun resides to
see where in life adventure is calling you.**

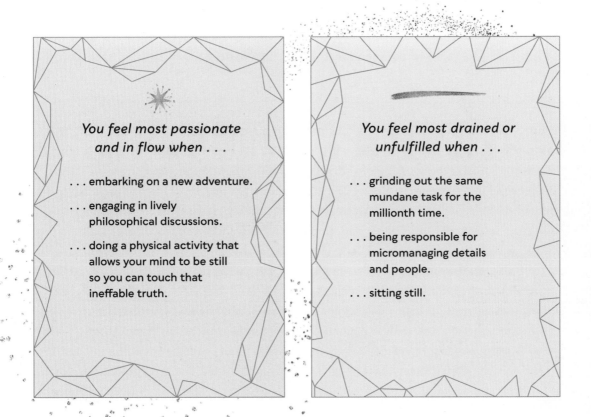

*You feel most passionate
and in flow when . . .*

. . . embarking on a new adventure.

. . . engaging in lively
philosophical discussions.

. . . doing a physical activity that
allows your mind to be still
so you can touch that
ineffable truth.

*You feel most drained or
unfulfilled when . . .*

. . . grinding out the same
mundane task for the
millionth time.

. . . being responsible for
micromanaging details
and people.

. . . sitting still.

SUN IN CAPRICORN

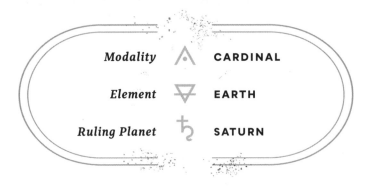

Modality	△	CARDINAL
Element	▽	EARTH
Ruling Planet	♄	SATURN

The essential drive of **CAPRICORN** is achievement. If there is a mountain to climb, Capricorn has mapped the route, packed the gear, and committed to the expedition. They are in it for the long haul. To achieve their goal, Capricorns call upon the attributes of their ruling planet, Saturn: discipline, responsibility, perseverance. Capricorn understands that achieving your dreams requires sacrifice and delayed gratification. It's no surprise that Capricorn Rising Jane Fonda popularized the axiom "no pain, no gain." Indeed, Capricorns instinctively understand that there's a certain satisfaction in self-denial or suffering in service of their goal.

Capricorns are least happy when there is no clear road to advancement. Because of this desire for demarcated career pathways, most Capricorns—depending on their other planetary placements— are comfortable in traditional professions and function well in established organizations and systems, following well-trodden paths. Because of this, they may be less apt to choose entrepreneurship or innovation even though they bear the initiatory energy of a cardinal sign.

Achievement is often something externally defined and validated, and that's generally acceptable to Capricorn. You may find yourself frustrated in your career, especially in entry-level positions, when there may be a lack of acknowledgment and rewards for your commitment and hard work. Knowing that goals and recognition for attaining them are core to your nature, how can you collaborate with your boss to build these into your work?

More than just the accolades, monetary rewards, and pleasure of accomplishment, you're interested in a legacy. What is the larger story of your work and contributions? This drive to create a body of work is another impetus for you to commit to a particular line of work rather than skip from one profession to another. Climbing to a summit takes time and dedication to a singular path. Switching tracks might be interesting for a mutable sign but likely frustrating and counterproductive for you.

In thinking about your life's purpose, your task is to get honest with yourself about what kinds of achievement matter to you. What metrics do you want to be evaluated by? What heights do you want to summit? What achievements do you want to be known for? Capricorns have an impressive tenacity and skill to accomplish anything, but finding a satisfying direction for that energy can be challenging.

Consider the house in which your Sun resides to see in which area of life you're most called to strive for achievement.

You feel most passionate and in flow when . . .

. . . working diligently toward your goal.

. . . tackling and completing a challenge that requires an immense amount of work and dedication.

. . . receiving recognition and just rewards for your hard work.

You feel most drained or unfulfilled when . . .

. . . your career doesn't offer clear pathways for advancement with defined milestones.

. . . your hard work and commitment aren't recognized and rewarded.

. . . work stagnates, becoming repetitive and lacking challenge.

SUN IN AQUARIUS

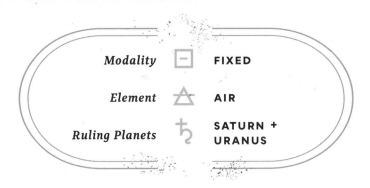

Modality	⊟	**FIXED**
Element	△	**AIR**
Ruling Planets	♄	**SATURN + URANUS**

The core energy of **AQUARIUS** is innovation. Aquarius can see that where we are now is a product of radical as well as incremental changes and so it is called to envision and create a new, better world. There is an inherent paradox to Aquarius that others—and even Aquarians themselves—may find confusing. While Aquarius, like its modern ruler Uranus, is a sign of revolution, modernization, and radical, progressive change, Aquarius also bears the traits of its traditional ruler, Saturn. Saturn is concerned with structure and stability. This dichotomous rulership imbues Aquarius with the ability to understand systems, while also realizing that they must always be tested, evaluated, and improved.

What enables Aquarius to be such a successful innovator is the ability to view problems with detachment. Aquarians can sometimes come off as cold and austere, unless their Moon or Rising signs strongly indicate affability (Leo, Sagittarius, Libra, Gemini) or prioritization of relationships and interpersonal connection (Cancer, Pisces). But this detachment is a superpower. It isn't that Aquarians do not have emotions, but they often hold the ability to separate themselves and view situations objectively. This is a valuable skill in their personal and professional lives.

While you may be concerned with starting revolutions, you also might just be interested in being an everyday rebel and marching to the beat of your own drum. Unlike every other planet in our solar system, Uranus is tilted on its axis so far that its equator is nearly at a right angle to its orbit. It's like it's rolling around the Sun on its side. Likewise, you may find that you're one of a kind, rolling through your orbit in your own unique fashion. This may make it difficult for you to relate and connect to others, but embracing and reveling in your individuality is part of your life's purpose. You show the rest of the zodiac that there isn't just one way to be. We can imagine new realities and then create them.

When considering your life's purpose, what work and experiences call to your curiosity and your drive to refine or disrupt current systems? What are the most satisfying problems you've solved? What revolution are you supporting? How are you leaving the world a better place than you found it? Most importantly, how are you embracing your individuality?

Consider the house in which your Sun resides to understand where in life you turn your discerning eye and where you seek to innovate change.

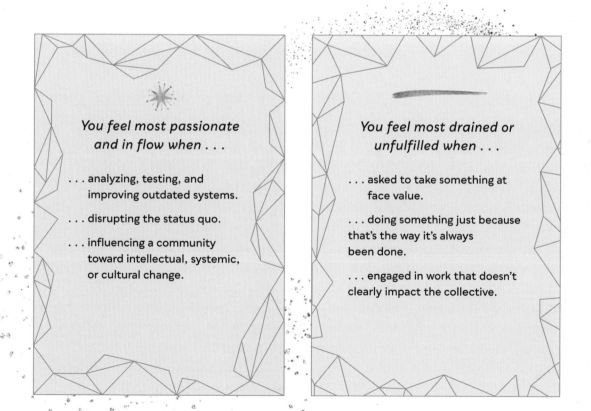

You feel most passionate and in flow when . . .

. . . analyzing, testing, and improving outdated systems.

. . . disrupting the status quo.

. . . influencing a community toward intellectual, systemic, or cultural change.

You feel most drained or unfulfilled when . . .

. . . asked to take something at face value.

. . . doing something just because that's the way it's always been done.

. . . engaged in work that doesn't clearly impact the collective.

SUN IN PISCES

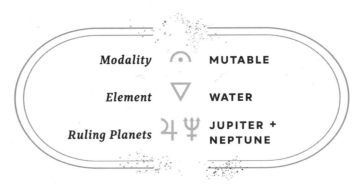

Modality	☉	**MUTABLE**
Element	▽	**WATER**
Ruling Planets	♃ ♆	**JUPITER + NEPTUNE**

50

PISCES is unbound water. It is diffuse, flowing freely, slipping into the cracks. Its nature is to be uncontained, so Piscean people may find it difficult to work in heavily structured environments. At the same time, having external structures ensuring accountability and methodical progress may be required for a Pisces to accomplish their lofty dreams—of which they have many. A blend of the optimism of its traditional ruler Jupiter and the dreamy intuition of its modern ruler Neptune, Pisces has a unique power to be the hopeful imagination of the collective. The benefits of this ability to channel the universal creative force is potent for any endeavor, from artist to healer to parent. The drawback can be a tendency to escapism from the suffocation of mundane human existence.

Pisces understands the illusion of man-made structures (language, law, government, social structures) and the sense of separation these structures create. They intuitively feel the connection between all people, of people to their environment, of everything energetically, of the material plane and the Divine. Pisces is perhaps the most spiritual sign of the zodiac. Even if they don't identify as religious or spiritual, Pisces has a keen awareness that there is something greater, be it art, humanity, the Earth, or some divine consciousness. Pisces is called to transcendent truth and isn't interested in or tethered to modern dogma about practicality, materialism, or arbitrary man-made rules. What can be difficult about this nature is that it doesn't fit well with Western capitalism, where your value as a person is often tied to what you produce and the quality of your life determined by how you monetize your time. The messages from society may make Pisces feel inadequate, lazy, or odd for not subscribing to mainstream values. But the nature of Pisces is a gift to myopic, fearful humanity that there is more to know, feel, and be beyond the scarcity mind-set of materialism. Piscean people can often be found as spiritual leaders, healers, or artists who help guide the rest of us beyond the limits of our perception. In this way, Pisces offers salvation from the tyranny of limiting beliefs and the isolation of modern life.

Consider the house in which your Sun resides to see where in life you most seek out the sense of connected oneness.

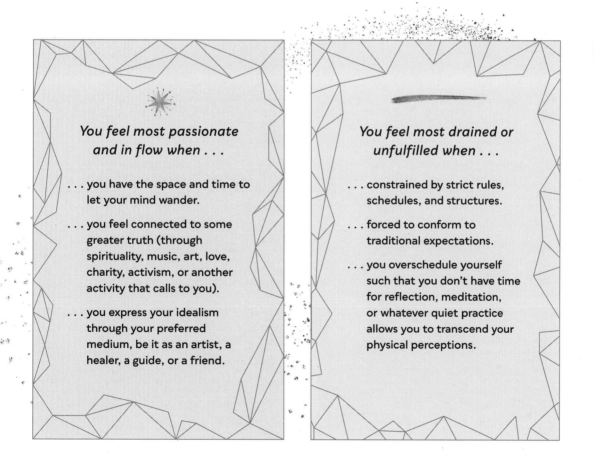

You feel most passionate and in flow when . . .

. . . you have the space and time to let your mind wander.

. . . you feel connected to some greater truth (through spirituality, music, art, love, charity, activism, or another activity that calls to you).

. . . you express your idealism through your preferred medium, be it as an artist, a healer, a guide, or a friend.

You feel most drained or unfulfilled when . . .

. . . constrained by strict rules, schedules, and structures.

. . . forced to conform to traditional expectations.

. . . you overschedule yourself such that you don't have time for reflection, meditation, or whatever quiet practice allows you to transcend your physical perceptions.

2

Your Sun House

WHERE YOU ARE ENERGIZED

The sign the Sun was in when you were born indicates the style in which you approach the world and live out your life's purpose. It's *how* you shine. The house your Sun resides in, on the other hand, speaks to *where* in life you shine and feel most energized. As discussed in **Understanding the Code**, there are twelve houses in a birth chart. Each house corresponds to certain domains of life. In this chapter, we will look at which house your natal Sun occupies to learn more about where in life you live out your purpose and the kinds of activities that most align to your purpose.

Let's get familiar with the house setup in your birth chart. The first thing to notice is that your Rising sign is always in the 1st House. The 2nd House is then occupied by the next sign in the zodiac, the 3rd House occupied by the sign after that, all the way through the twelve signs of the zodiac. For example, if your Rising sign is Gemini, then your 1st House will be occupied by Gemini, your 2nd House will be occupied by Cancer, your 3rd House occupied by Leo, and so on.

IDENTIFYING YOUR RISING SIGN

Your Rising sign is the zodiacal sign containing your Ascendant point. Remember that the Ascendant point is the position of the eastern horizon at the moment of your birth. Imagine a line being drawn from the eastern horizon out into space and connecting with a specific degree of a zodiacal sign—for example, 12 degrees of Libra; that exact degree is the Ascendant point and establishes the Rising sign as Libra. The Rising sign always occupies the 1st House, so in your birth chart, your Ascendant point (abbreviated as AC) should always appear somewhere in your 1st House.

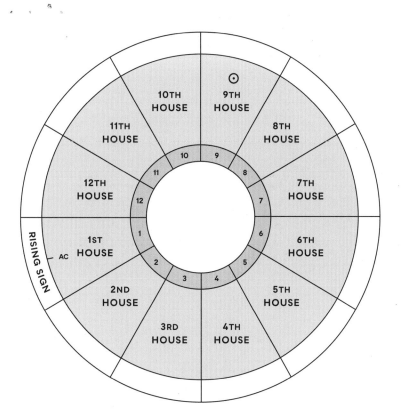

YOUR SUN HOUSE

DECODING HOUSE PLACEMENTS

Your Sun house is a key component in understanding which topics in life are central to your life's purpose, but it's only one part of the story. Understanding the house your Rising sign ruler is placed in (chapter 4) and the house your Moon occupies (chapter 6) are also important considerations for which areas of life are most critical for you. After reading about those three placements, you can blend and balance the meaning of those houses. See the final section, **Calibration**, for an example.

Where the Sun, Moon, and planets were in the sky at the moment you were born are mapped out on your birth chart, falling into specific signs and houses. Each planetary placement has some meaning about your personality and life's purpose. In this chapter, we're focusing on the meaning of your Sun's house placement. The Sun could be placed in any house in your chart and that placement describes what places in life you feel most energized, alive, and in flow.

This chapter covers in depth the meaning of the Sun's placement in each of the twelve houses, but the following chart gives a quick overview of the house meanings for your reference.

As you read through the description for your Sun's house, consider those domains of life. How have they been important to you? When you engage in these aspects of your life, do you feel in flow? How does the style of your Sun sign influence these aspects of life? How do these aspects of your life give your life meaning and purpose? How has your relationship to these house topics developed over time?

After reading your Sun sign and Sun house descriptions, check out **Cracking the Code: Your Core Self** for more guided reflection on the meaning of your natal Sun.

HOUSE MEANINGS

HOUSE	MEANING
1	Self and identity
2	Money, assets, and skills
3	Communication, local community, and siblings
4	Home, family, and lineage
5	Creativity and children
6	Daily work, habits, and health
7	Collaboration and committed partnership
8	Shared resources, endings, and transformation
9	Learning, teaching, spirituality, and travel
10	Career and public life
11	Communities, friends, and patrons
12	Hidden life, your unconscious mind, and connection to the Divine

YOUR SUN HOUSE

Fill in the blanks with information from your own birth chart
and referring to the House Meanings chart.

Your Sun house: _____

Parts of life signified by that house: _____

SUN IN THE 1st HOUSE

SELF AND IDENTITY

The **1st HOUSE** is the house of self. It is the house of personal identity, self-actualization, and your physical body and appearance. It is the house of *you*. When your Sun resides in the 1st House, your life's purpose requires that you, personally, shine. Your purpose is to focus on self. You are here to self-actualize and self-express. Your art, your voice, your ideas are meant to be heard. This doesn't necessarily mean that your audience will be the whole world and that you live a very public life. Rather, it's that your life's purpose is about living and expressing authentically. There is a calling for you, in this life, to prioritize yourself.

Perhaps this resonates with you and you feel comfortable taking up space and shining your light. Huzzah! But for many with this placement, there is discomfort in prioritizing themselves. For some, calling attention to themselves has meant inviting danger. For others, particularly mothers, there is an internalized narrative that self-effacement and martyrdom are required to be deemed good and worthy. It may very well be critical to your life's purpose to overcome these oppressive beliefs. Something that may help you is to realize that shining your light and deeming yourself worthy to be seen, heard, and valued is the contribution you make to the collective. By claiming and valuing yourself, you model for others that they are worthy and valuable, too. That they can take up space, too. That they matter just like YOU matter, as you are, flaws and all. Your passions, thoughts, art, enthusiasm, struggles, and triumphs are all important and central to your life's work. In this life, you are called to focus on yourself.

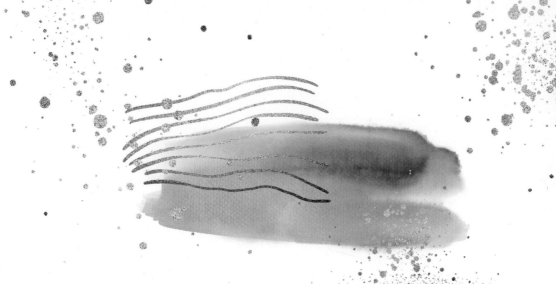

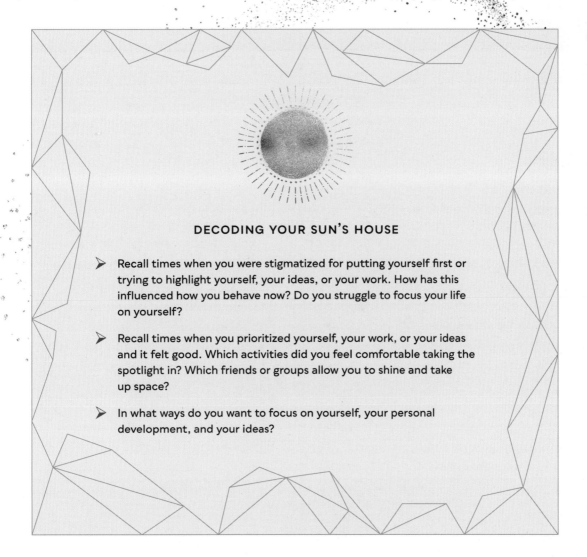

DECODING YOUR SUN'S HOUSE

➤ Recall times when you were stigmatized for putting yourself first or trying to highlight yourself, your ideas, or your work. How has this influenced how you behave now? Do you struggle to focus your life on yourself?

➤ Recall times when you prioritized yourself, your work, or your ideas and it felt good. Which activities did you feel comfortable taking the spotlight in? Which friends or groups allow you to shine and take up space?

➤ In what ways do you want to focus on yourself, your personal development, and your ideas?

SUN IN THE 2ND HOUSE

MONEY, ASSETS, AND SKILLS

The **2ND HOUSE** pertains to your money and assets, how you manage them, and the skills with which you acquire money and assets. With your Sun in the 2nd House, your life's purpose is intertwined with your profession. Certainly, for most of us, our jobs play a large role in our lives, often demanding a majority of our time and energy. But for you especially, making and managing your own money, and the satisfaction and autonomy that comes with that, will be a central theme in your life.

This placement means that self-expressing in the style of your Sun sign will be your key strategy for making money. For example, if your Sun is in Leo in the 2nd House, your work will likely include some kind of performance, perhaps as an actor, teacher, writer, or some other mode of artistic expression. Equally, though, Leo Sun in the 2nd House could express as a charismatic employee in any role, like as a bartender, wedding planner, or CEO. The idea is that your charisma is the critical skill in whatever job you do. Alternatively, if you have your Sun in Cancer in the 2nd House, your key skill for making money will likely entail caregiving, nurturing, or relationship building. Read more about your Sun sign (chapter 1) for additional information on the style in which you make money.

Having your Sun in the 2nd House usually speaks to a notable ability to make money. If your Sun is in a mutable sign (Gemini, Virgo, Pisces, or Sagittarius), you may find yourself with multiple revenue streams at once, like a primary job and a side hustle. The key idea is that you, your vibrancy, and your core nature are intimately tied to how you make money.

Having your Sun in the 2nd House also means that managing your money and being financially independent are central to your life's purpose. For some people, their fortunes are tied up with others, but for you, standing on your own financially will be energizing and empowering.

FIND OUT MORE

Your Sun is placed in one of your Houses of Substance. You can read more about these houses in your chart in part IV.

59

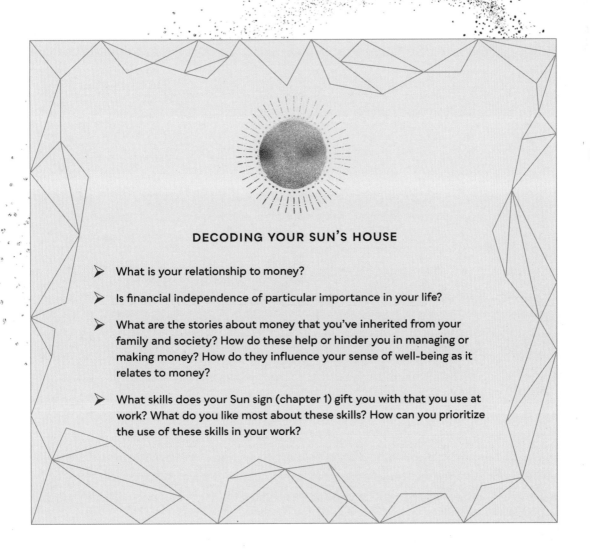

DECODING YOUR SUN'S HOUSE

➢ What is your relationship to money?

➢ Is financial independence of particular importance in your life?

➢ What are the stories about money that you've inherited from your family and society? How do these help or hinder you in managing or making money? How do they influence your sense of well-being as it relates to money?

➢ What skills does your Sun sign (chapter 1) gift you with that you use at work? What do you like most about these skills? How can you prioritize the use of these skills in your work?

SUN IN THE 3RD HOUSE

COMMUNICATION, LOCAL COMMUNITY, AND SIBLINGS

60

With your Sun in the **3RD House**, communication will be a central theme of your life's purpose. You have something to say, wisdom to share, a drive to entertain, or a talent for mediation. Look to your Sun sign to give you more information about the style and content of what you're here to communicate.

This placement generally speaks to an inquisitive nature that lives to follow ideas down the rabbit hole and get lost in whatever your current obsession is, and then to share about that obsession. People with this placement may become teachers, especially primary or secondary school teachers, as this house relates to the education we receive in our early life.

Any form of communicating ideas is the purview of the 3rd House. The key to unlocking the power of the 3rd House Sun is understanding the strengths and style of your Sun sign and how that indicates what you're passionate about communicating and how. A Libra 3rd House Sun might work well in verbal or writing communications—e.g., dialogue, diplomacy, and coaching—on Venusian topics like aesthetics, culture, relationships, or justice. A Pisces 3rd House Sun may be looking to communicate about spirituality and through emotionally evocative, nonverbal expressions, like visual or performing arts. It will be vital for you to test out different communication methods to figure out what feels best and most in alignment. Through trial, error, and experience, you'll come to find the topics and ways of communicating that are most fulfilling and help you connect with your audience.

COMMUNICATION STYLE BY 3RD HOUSE SIGN

Your communication style is . . .

Aries	Fast and combative	**Libra**	Informed and charming
Taurus	Laid-back and down-to-earth	**Scorpio**	Intense and incisive
Gemini	Frantic and informative	**Sagittarius**	Fun and philosophical
Cancer	Comforting and inclusive	**Capricorn**	Pragmatic and concrete
Leo	Performative and enthusiastic	**Aquarius**	Insightful and innovative
Virgo	Clear and discerning	**Pisces**	Compassionate and dreamy

DECODING YOUR SUN'S HOUSE

➤ What messages or wisdom do you want to share?

➤ What is your favorite means of communication (e.g., written, verbal, abstract visuals, metaphor, music)?

➤ What do you want to learn and what do you want to teach?

SUN IN THE 4TH HOUSE

HOME, FAMILY, AND LINEAGE

The **4TH HOUSE** is the place of home and family in our charts. It speaks to our childhood home, as well as the home we cultivate for ourselves as adults. It also describes our family, both our family of origin and chosen family. It is the house that speaks of our parents, our lineage, and where we come from. When your Sun resides in your 4th House, you are energized and enlivened in your home space. It is likely your sanctuary. You may find that you work best from home, or that the cultivation of home and family life is central to your life's purpose.

You may find that in your work, the topic of home, homeland, and lineage may be most meaningful to you. Perhaps cultivating home and family for others through social work or the healing of familial wounds as a therapist call to you. Work to do with tracing ancestry, immigration rights, or the preservation of cultural heritage could resonate with your 4th House Sun energy. Perhaps you are an artist, and your work interrogates the ideas of home, family, and ancestors. There are many expressions of 4th House Sun energy, so don't feel confined to interpretations that only focus on your physical home or nuclear family.

The 4th House is our most private, personal space. It serves as the foundation that supports the whole of your life. Do you shine best in private? Are you most yourself and alive when at home or with family? Even if your Sun is in the 4th House, you also have a 10th House (see part IV) and a public life. You may still have a very public-facing professional life. But this Sun placement speaks to the centrality of home to your soul's purpose and where you are energized.

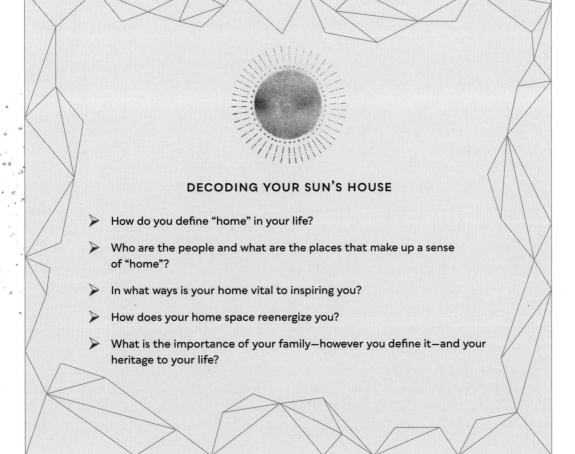

DECODING YOUR SUN'S HOUSE

➤ How do you define "home" in your life?

➤ Who are the people and what are the places that make up a sense of "home"?

➤ In what ways is your home vital to inspiring you?

➤ How does your home space reenergize you?

➤ What is the importance of your family—however you define it—and your heritage to your life?

SUN IN THE 5th HOUSE

CREATIVITY AND CHILDREN

The **5th HOUSE** corresponds to our creative expression. It is the place of our creative works and of children (the creative expression of our bodies). Having your natal Sun in the 5th House means that you are energized by and feel in flow when engaging with your creativity and cultivating your creative works. Your children, your book babies, your art portfolio, your music, your crafts, your start-up—likely a combination of several creative outlets—are what make you feel most alive. It isn't that people with their Suns in other houses don't create (we all have a 5th House in our charts), but for you it is the act of creating that makes you feel most invigorated and is central to your life's purpose.

The 5th House sign can give us insights into the nature of our creative expressions and what inspires us. See the Creativity Style by 5th House Sign chart for a quick guide, or dig into your Sun sign (chapter 1) for more insights on the style of your creativity. Remember that creativity is not confined to artistic expression or craftwork. There is creativity in everything from day-to-day problem solving, to workplace collaborations, to decorating your desk. Find the creative outlets that call to you and allow you to express your Sun sign style.

For some with this placement, being a parent or working with and caring for children can be central to their life's purpose. Note that creativity and caregiving can be a both/and, not either/or situation. A 5th House Sun person can gain fulfillment and fully express their chart as a parent as well as a creator. Alternatively, you may focus on caregiving or on your creative works and not both. Feel into what calls to you.

CREATIVITY STYLE BY 5TH HOUSE SIGN

Your creativity is marked by . . .

Aries	Speed, aggression, and passion	**Libra**	Harmony, balance, and justice
Taurus	Beauty, sensuality, and engaging one or more of the five senses	**Scorpio**	Emotional intensity and shock value
Gemini	Multiplicity, ingenuity, and curiosity	**Sagittarius**	Philosophical inquiry, cultural exchange, and optimism
Cancer	Compassion, emotional connection, and nostalgia	**Capricorn**	Structure, restraint, and timelessness
Leo	Self-expression, enthusiasm, and magnanimity	**Aquarius**	Innovation, detachment, and eccentricity
Virgo	Precision, perfection, and problem solving	**Pisces**	Surrealism, spirituality, and interconnectivity

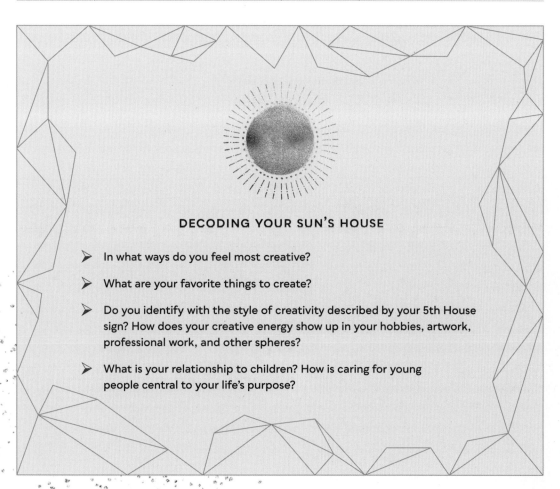

DECODING YOUR SUN'S HOUSE

➤ In what ways do you feel most creative?

➤ What are your favorite things to create?

➤ Do you identify with the style of creativity described by your 5th House sign? How does your creative energy show up in your hobbies, artwork, professional work, and other spheres?

➤ What is your relationship to children? How is caring for young people central to your life's purpose?

SUN IN THE 6TH HOUSE

DAILY WORK, HABITS, AND HEALTH

The **6TH HOUSE** encompasses our day-to-day work and habits. Having your Sun in the 6th House indicates that you are energized by and in flow with your day-to-day work. You'll feel especially in flow when your daily work is structured in the style of your 6th House sign. A Pisces 6th House Sun may require ample time for daydreaming, spirituality, and artistic expression without a rigid structure, whereas a Virgo 6th House Sun will thrive on deadlines and to-do lists. (Read about your Sun sign in chapter 1 and more on your 6th House in part IV to get a better sense of how your 6th House sign wants to express itself in your day-to-day work.) It may seem odd to say that you truly shine in the daily grind, but what this means is that the work itself is as fulfilling as the completion of a project.

Alternatively, Sun in the 6th House can simply mean that you feel most energized and in flow when you structure your daily life in a way that resonates with your core style (Sun sign), so not necessarily just the work that you do every day, but also your morning rituals, your regular health habits, or your coffee rituals. For example, if your 6th House sign is Taurus, having daily rituals that prioritize sensual pleasures like cooking delicious food or enjoying a luxuriant skin care routine could be part of your core nature and how you live out your life's purpose. Remember that we aren't just here to create some major body of work or accomplish huge goals. We are also here to enjoy each moment and the beauty of everyday life—and no one more so than a person with their Sun in the 6th House.

The 6th House is also concerned with your physical health, which in large part is the result of your daily habits. Having your Sun in the 6th House may indicate that your life's purpose will involve a focus on your physical well-being, or perhaps the well-being of others. Because of the ties to physical health, people with their Sun in the 6th House may find their vocation in the health care industry or other healing modalities.

FIND OUT MORE

Your Sun is placed in one of your Houses of Substance. You can read more about these houses in your chart in part IV.

DECODING YOUR SUN'S HOUSE

➤ What is most fulfilling about your day-to-day work?

➤ How can you prioritize what aspects are more engrossing and minimize what is most tedious?

➤ How does the style of your 6th House sign inform how you structure your day-to-day work and routines? In what ways could you align your daily routines to your 6th House sign to feel more in flow?

➤ How do you prioritize maintaining your health in your daily rituals? Is health care or healing of interest to you professionally?

SUN IN THE 7TH HOUSE

COLLABORATION AND COMMITTED PARTNERSHIP

The **7TH HOUSE** is the house of committed partnership, most especially long-term, committed romantic, platonic, and business relationships. There is a contractual element to these relationships, whether the contracts are legally binding or socially constructed. For example, marriage is a legally contracted relationship, but a long-term platonic relationship with a friend is also subject to rules, obligations, and expectations, likely agreed to implicitly as much as explicitly.

People with their natal Sun in the 7th House shine best in collaboration. This could take many forms in a person's life. You could feel a sense of flow and fulfillment in your committed romantic relationships. Perhaps you and your romantic partner even own a business together, or being in a healthy, supportive relationship is essential for you to express your full potential. This isn't to say that people with 7th House Suns always have great, healthy romantic relationships, but rather that cultivating healthy long-term committed partnerships (romantic, platonic, or business) will enable you to shine best. Indeed, it may benefit a 7th House Sun to have a collection of committed relationships (e.g., business clients and a romantic partner) so that your full self-expression doesn't weigh too heavily on any one relationship.

The strength of this position is that you are great at connecting with others one-on-one. Your methods for doing this are described by your Sun sign (chapter 1). Connecting and collaborating with people as a coach, boss, business colleague, advocate, or friend is your gift. The challenge of this position is that you may become lost in the other, putting others first to an excessive degree or relying on them codependently for your well-being or life meaning. You are not only your Sun sign and house. You are a whole, complex, wonderful birth chart. See this placement as your unique gift to connect with others meaningfully and productively, rather than as a need for partnership, and you'll avoid the trap of staying in relationships you should leave or seeking out any relationship just to have one.

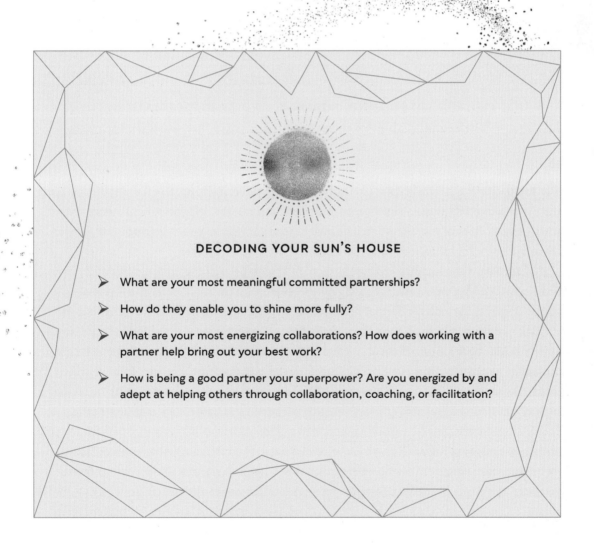

DECODING YOUR SUN'S HOUSE

➤ What are your most meaningful committed partnerships?

➤ How do they enable you to shine more fully?

➤ What are your most energizing collaborations? How does working with a partner help bring out your best work?

➤ How is being a good partner your superpower? Are you energized by and adept at helping others through collaboration, coaching, or facilitation?

SUN IN THE 8TH HOUSE

SHARED RESOURCES, ENDINGS, AND TRANSFORMATION

The **8TH HOUSE** is a complex place in the birth chart. On the one hand, it is the part of your chart that deals with other people's money or shared assets: loans, taxes, inheritances, or money shared with a spouse. To have your natal Sun here might mean you're drawn to managing other people's money or assets, for example as an agent, a financial advisor, or a realtor.

The 8th House also signifies some of the more difficult aspects of the human experience. It is the place of death, transformation, and rebirth. People with their Sun in the 8th House may also be drawn to the topics of death. This can show up professionally as a hospice nurse, but also through more artistic avenues such as a writer whose books interrogate the concept of mortality. More broadly, the 8th House is about endings and the transformations that must happen before something new can begin. A plant lives its life, dies, and is transformed through decomposition into fertile soil from which new life grows. There are many ways that you might engage with the topic of transformation as part of your life's purpose. Perhaps you are called to facilitate other people's transformations as a counselor, serving as a guide while one part of someone's journey ends and a new adventure begins. Perhaps you create immersive, transformative experiences through performance art. Related to death and endings, the 8th House is also the place of mental health and grief. You might feel called to support others through mental health issues, perhaps as a grief counselor, psychiatrist, or addiction therapist. There are innumerable endings and beginnings in our lives, and something about this liminal, transitional space calls to you.

These topics will call to you and your Sun sign (chapter 1) will guide the manner in which you engage with them. There is a tendency in our society to shy away from difficult topics like death and mental illness, but they are essential parts of being human and not to be feared. Indeed, you have a unique ability to sit with these aspects of human experience. It is a gift you can cultivate, in whatever way feels most true to you.

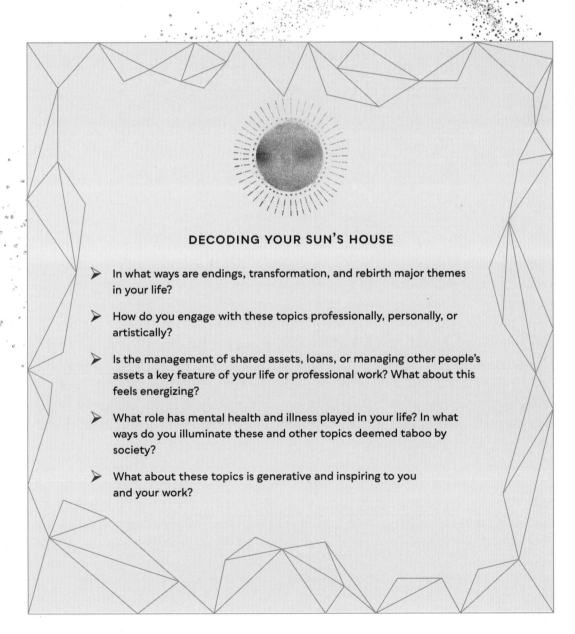

DECODING YOUR SUN'S HOUSE

➤ In what ways are endings, transformation, and rebirth major themes in your life?

➤ How do you engage with these topics professionally, personally, or artistically?

➤ Is the management of shared assets, loans, or managing other people's assets a key feature of your life or professional work? What about this feels energizing?

➤ What role has mental health and illness played in your life? In what ways do you illuminate these and other topics deemed taboo by society?

➤ What about these topics is generative and inspiring to you and your work?

SUN IN THE 9TH HOUSE

LEARNING, TEACHING, SPIRITUALITY, AND TRAVEL

72

The primary energy of the **9TH HOUSE** is the call to seek and understand. It is the place of learning, teaching, writing, and publishing. All manner of intellectual inquiry lives here, including traditional higher education as well as personal approach to study. All domains of study live here as well, from core subject areas to esoteric philosophy and religion. It is a house concerned with the seeking and sharing of knowledge. Perhaps you cultivate a life of study, whether formally in academia or informally as a voracious reader or student of human nature. What is it that you want to know? There is always another rabbit hole to fall into and you are insatiable. How can you create more space and opportunity to learn? You may feel called to work as a teacher, writer, podcaster—any outlet to share your knowledge. Alternatively, you may find satisfaction working in the industries of education, publishing, travel, or journalism. Because this is the house that relates to spiritual studies, you may find that a major part of your life's purpose involves spiritual inquiry and practice.

The seeking drive of the 9th House often spurs people with their Sun sign here to travel far and wide. Your thirst for understanding leads you to new locales and foreign shores. You know that there are certain understandings that can only be captured through direct experience, and not just in a book. You have an intrepid spirit and are always hearing the call of adventure whispered to your spirit.

APPROACHES TO INQUIRY BY 9TH HOUSE SIGN ELEMENT

In your learning and adventures, you desire . . .

Earth	tangible data and results
Air	philosophical discussions and intellectual rigor
Water	intuitive and spiritual approaches to wisdom
Fire	action-oriented and experiential inquiry

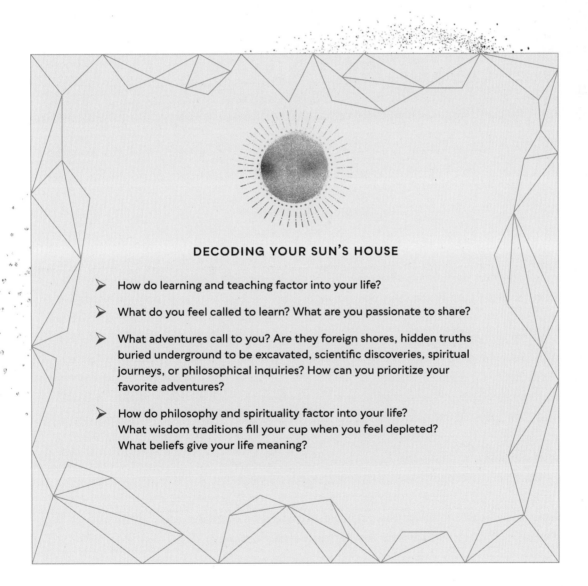

DECODING YOUR SUN'S HOUSE

➤ How do learning and teaching factor into your life?

➤ What do you feel called to learn? What are you passionate to share?

➤ What adventures call to you? Are they foreign shores, hidden truths buried underground to be excavated, scientific discoveries, spiritual journeys, or philosophical inquiries? How can you prioritize your favorite adventures?

➤ How do philosophy and spirituality factor into your life? What wisdom traditions fill your cup when you feel depleted? What beliefs give your life meaning?

SUN IN THE 10TH HOUSE

CAREER AND PUBLIC LIFE

The **10TH HOUSE** is the place of career and public life in our charts. It is the highest point in our charts, the most visible place, the zenith. While the 2nd and 6th Houses also speak to our work lives, the 10th House is about the totality of our career, the big picture, and what we accomplish in our public lives (see **Part IV: Your Work** for more). To have your natal Sun here means that you shine most brightly in your career or in the public sphere. It is a strong signature for fame, with many prominent individuals having their Sun here: Toni Morrison, Al Pacino, Paul McCartney, Gwen Stefani, Lauryn Hill, Martha Stewart, Whoopi Goldberg, and Paul Rudd. This placement doesn't mean that you have to seek fame to the level these individuals did, but rather that you could. The essential meaning of Sun in the 10th House is that you shine most authentically and vibrantly through your career. Your Sun sign gives further information about the style of career most suited to you (see chapter 1).

What can be liberating about accepting your 10th House Sun is that you can embrace your commitment to your work or the public notoriety you seek. Other people may not get it—they aren't 10th House Suns. But to you, your career is where you express your soul. You are passionate about it and finding the right fit is central to your life's purpose.

A challenge for you may be finding that work-life balance. The 10th House is opposite the 4th House of home and family, which illustrates the tension between our public and private lives, our career and our family. It is not impossible to find a balance, though. The 4th House of family is the most private place in our chart; it is the place of our physical home and our family life. It can be seen as the foundation of our charts, where we are rooted and supported. Being able to cultivate a solid home space can be key in enabling you to have the energy and support needed to shine your 10th House Sun in whatever career and public sphere you choose.

FIND OUT MORE

Your Sun is placed in one of your Houses of Substance. You can read more about these houses in your chart in part IV.

DECODING YOUR SUN'S HOUSE

➤ What is your relationship to work and your career?

➤ Has it been central to your life, or would you like it to be more so?

➤ Do you feel you commit too much time to your career, to the detriment of other aspects of your life?

➤ What narratives have you internalized about career? Do they help or hinder you from committing the time and resources necessary to build a satisfying career?

➤ What is your relationship to fame? What notoriety do you seek? Do you find it easy to take a role in the spotlight? What kind of fame entices you?

SUN IN THE 11TH HOUSE

COMMUNITIES, FRIENDS, AND PATRONS

The **11TH HOUSE** is the place of friends, groups, community, clients, fans, and patrons. It is the place of all groups of people, from your intimate friend groups to humanity as a whole. Having your natal Sun here means you are energized by bringing people together, organizing groups, shining before your fans, or engaging in professions that focus on building a client base. You are the community builder. Look to the sign of your Sun for information about the style in which you engage with the collective (see chart on next page, as well as chapter 1).

Perhaps you feel like you are too introverted to be an 11th House Sun, but on the most basic level, this placement means you shine where you belong. That could be building an online community, connecting with fans of your work on a platform like Patreon, or feeling most fulfilled in your close-knit friend group. On the other hand, you may embrace your natural community-building skills to cultivate a fan base and seek fame. Some notable 11th House Suns include Marilyn Monroe, Marcel Marceau, Jim Morrison, and John Elway.

This placement could inspire you to be of service to humanity more broadly. Advocacy, community organizing, and activism may be your calling. You understand that we are all connected and accountable to one another. This isn't a burden, but an opportunity. You remind us all that we are in this together, which is a comfort but also a responsibility.

COMMUNICATION STYLE BY 11TH HOUSE SIGN

You build and support community by . . .

Aries	Championing and defending others	**Libra**	Creating beauty, harmony, peace, and justice for others
Taurus	Creating sumptuous experiences for others	**Scorpio**	Facilitating transformative experiences for others
Gemini	Engaging others in thoughtful, provocative conversation	**Sagittarius**	Inspiring optimism and adventure
Cancer	Caretaking others and building a sense of family	**Capricorn**	Creating lasting structures and building toward tangible results
Leo	Attracting fans and clients through your performance	**Aquarius**	Sparking innovation or rebellion to create a new reality
Virgo	Serving the needs of your communities by solving problems	**Pisces**	Creating meaningful, perhaps spiritual connections among people and with some greater ideal

DECODING YOUR SUN'S HOUSE

➤ In what groups do you feel most alive?

➤ What communities do you identify with and how does engaging with them nurture and energize you?

➤ What is it about you that brings people together? How does this resonate with your Sun sign?

➤ What communities do you want to serve and support? How do you want to bring people together for the greater good?

SUN IN THE 12TH HOUSE

HIDDEN LIFE, YOUR UNCONSCIOUS MIND, AND CONNECTION TO THE DIVINE

The **12TH HOUSE** is the place of that which is hidden: secrets, your unconscious mind, the collective unconscious, the spiritual realms. Your natal Sun shining here seeks to illuminate these hidden places. People with this placement are often deeply spiritual and feel a connection with the Divine, however they define it. A Taurus Sun in the 12th House may feel a deep connection to the Earth and the cycles of the seasons, whereas a Pisces Sun in the 12th House may feel a psychic connection to other realms. Indeed, anyone with their Sun in the 12th House may have marked psychic abilities because they are illuminating unseen, hidden places.

This Sun placement is about bringing to light suppressed, unconscious material, either your personal hidden psychological mind or the collective unconscious mind. You may have a lifelong obsession with personal introspection. What revelations, what art, what compassion does this self-inquiry inspire in you? Additionally, you could feel tapped into the collective unconscious, weaving stories featuring universal, archetypal themes or serving as a mouthpiece for the zeitgeist. How you tap into this unconscious material will vary from person to person, but keeping track of your dreams, allowing time for your imagination to wander, and developing a meditation practice could be particularly potent practices in support of your unconscious excavations.

You could also have a passion for uncovering the hidden. I once gave an astrology reading to an individual with a 12th House Sun who was filming a documentary on forgotten towns and peoples. What is hidden or forgotten that you want to spotlight?

This placement may mean that you feel most in flow when in isolation, doing whatever activities make you feel most fulfilled (see your Sun sign in chapter 1 for more insights into what activities energize you). This isn't to say you dislike social interactions, but rather that you are more vital and expressive in solitude. Perhaps you create your best work when left alone to your own thoughts.

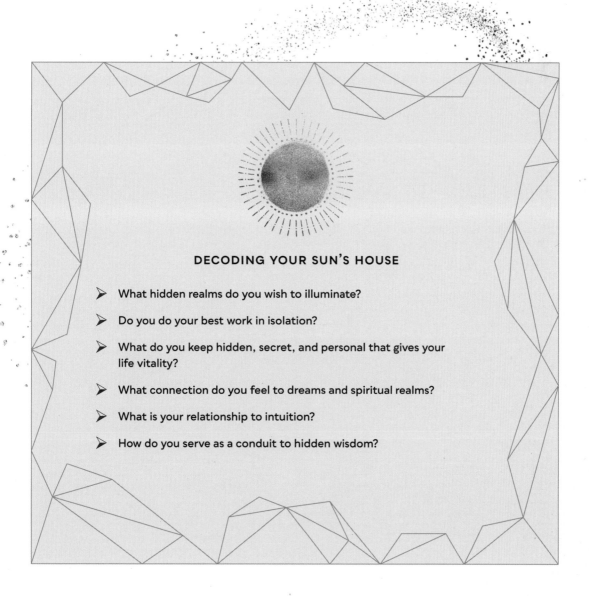

DECODING YOUR SUN'S HOUSE

➤ What hidden realms do you wish to illuminate?

➤ Do you do your best work in isolation?

➤ What do you keep hidden, secret, and personal that gives your life vitality?

➤ What connection do you feel to dreams and spiritual realms?

➤ What is your relationship to intuition?

➤ How do you serve as a conduit to hidden wisdom?

DECODING THE STARS

ALBERT EINSTEIN

BIRTH DATE: March 14, 1879
BIRTH TIME: 11:30 a.m.
BIRTH LOCATION: Ulm, Germany

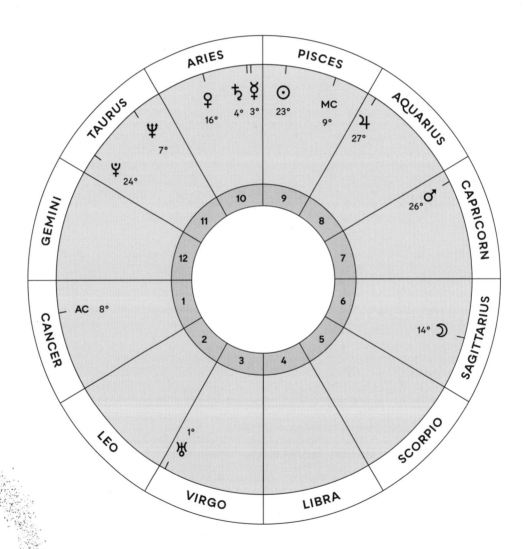

ALBERT EINSTEIN was born with his natal Sun in Pisces in the 9th House. The Sun in the 9th House can signify someone who shines and is most energized by scholarship, study, research, publishing, and teaching. A Nobel Prize–winning physicist, author of several books and more than 140 journal articles, a professor, and considered to be the most influential physicist of the 20th century, Einstein fully expressed his 9th House Sun energy.

Understanding how he expressed his Pisces Sun energy may seem less obvious. Pisces is a sign of dreams, imagination, artistry, intuition, and spirituality. Pisces understands the relationship of the micro to the macro, the individual to the universe, and that there is some larger, unseen architecture underlying all things. Pisces strives to understand and experience those great truths, using their intuition as a way to connect with the Divine.

In his work, Einstein sought to understand the nature of the universe and express that truth through the language of mathematics and physics. Like a true Pisces, he wasn't hampered by conventional wisdom or the scientific establishment, but rather relied on his imagination to guide him to revolutionary ways of thinking and groundbreaking theories. In a 1929 interview with *The Saturday Evening Post*, Einstein stressed the importance of intuition and inspiration in his process. He believed that knowledge is limited, and that imagination is necessary to dream up new theories to test. He likened his work to that of an artist, rather than a scientist only. In these ideas, we can see the influence of his Piscean nature on his approach to the 9th House work. Another physicist with a 9th House Sun in another zodiacal sign would likely have a different worldview and experience. And yet without interviews and autobiographical reflections, how would we get this insight into the true nature of Einstein and his approach to his life's work? Being a physicist and trying to develop a unified theory that would describe the inherent connection between all things was a means of expressing his Piscean nature. The central quality of Pisces is a desire to dissolve boundaries and reveal how all things are interrelated.

When you decode your Sun sign and house, the most important information it provides is the core qualities of your nature that are then expressed in all you do, rather than indicating some specific task. Finding work, hobbies, and relationships that allow you to fully express your core nature is a key part in identifying your life's purpose.

CRACKING THE CODE
YOUR CORE SELF

YOUR SUN SIGN

*What parts of your Sun sign
description resonate with you?*

How do you shine? What energizes you?

----

*What activities in your personal or professional
life resonate with your Sun sign style?*

YOUR SUN HOUSE

*When considering your Sun house,
how do you shine in those areas of life?*

----

*What activities in your personal or
professional life resonate with the topics of
your Sun house placement?*

----

*When have you felt in flow during activities that
correspond to your Sun house?*

82

SIGN + HOUSE

When and where do you feel most in flow?
What activities are most satisfying, even if they are a struggle to complete?
How do these activities resonate with your Sun sign and house?
How can you allocate more time and energy to these activities?

83

When do you feel most depleted?
How do these activities seem misaligned to your Sun sign and house?
How can you reduce these kinds of activities in your life?

PART II

YOUR MOTIVATION

THE SUN IS YOUR CORE ESSENCE, your vital energetic signature, and the gravitational force around which your other attributes revolve. How (your Sun sign) and where (your Sun house) you shine and feel energized influence what actions you feel called to take in this life. But your birth chart gives much more information about what motivates you and what you are here to do. As unique and complex as each individual, a birth chart is a rich tapestry of information. After understanding your Sun placement, the next major facet of your chart to decode is your Rising sign.

The **Rising sign** refers to the zodiacal sign ascending over the eastern horizon at the moment of your birth. The Sun rises in the east, initiating the day. Likewise, the Rising sign speaks to the energy that incites you to action. Your Rising sign is what drives you. But where are you being driven? The house placement of your **Rising sign ruler** describes where your life is being steered.

In this part, we'll dive into your Rising sign and the Rising sign ruler's placement to unpack the intricacies of your motivation and life direction.

Your Rising Sign

WHAT MOTIVATES YOU

YOUR RISING SIGN is a deeply personal aspect of your birth chart. The Sun remains in the same sign for about thirty days, but the Rising sign changes every two hours as the Earth swiftly rotates on its axis. So while everyone born within a thirty-day period will have the same Sun sign, the Rising sign is quickly shifting. As you took your first breath, your life apart from your mother began. You became an individual. And that sign rising over the eastern horizon speaks to that initiatory energy. What incites and motivates you is encapsulated in the Rising sign.

Ancient Hellenistic astrologers referred to the Rising sign as the "helm" of the chart—the helm being the place from which a ship is steered. Your Rising sign speaks to the energy, topics, and actions that motivate and direct you. In this chapter, we'll consider your Rising sign, your motivation, and its impact on your life's purpose.

The Rising sign is so critical to your personal astrology that it is what sets up the whole organization of your birth chart. The Rising sign always occupies the 1st House in a chart, and every successive house is occupied by the subsequent sign in the zodiac. Looking at your birth chart, identify your 1st House and note the zodiacal sign that occupies it.

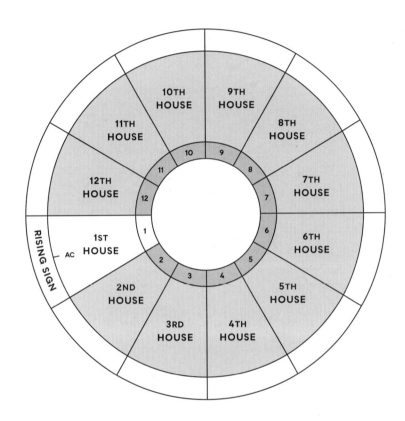

Just as with the Sun sign, we need to consider two aspects of your Rising sign: its element and modality.

The **element** of your Rising sign describes whether your motivation is:

▽ **EARTH**   material security and tangible accomplishments

△ **AIR**   intellectual curiosity and communication

▽ **WATER**   meaningful relationships, emotional security, and intimacy

△ **FIRE**   freedom to live your life and enact your will

The **modality** of your Rising sign indicates whether you are motivated to:

CARDINAL   initiate action and lead

FIXED   stabilize situations and persist

MUTABLE   be energized by liminality and serve as an agent of change

When thinking about times that you felt most motivated, how did the element and modality of your Rising sign come into play? When reading through your Rising sign description, consider how the sign's element and modality influence your motivation in your day-to-day life. For example, if you are a Scorpio Rising (water/fixed), how are you motivated to hold, sustain, and persist? In what ways are you tireless? In what ways are you stubborn? How do your emotional intelligence, intuition, and emotional connections direct and motivate your life? Astrology memes may joke about Scorpio's intensity in digging for the deepest, darkest secrets of others, but their indefatigable tenacity is an expression of the fixed nature of the sign, and the need for emotional honesty is an expression of its water element. How do your modality and element show up for you?

Beyond the element and modality, each individual sign describes different motivating factors. When reading the entry for your Rising sign, what resonates and what doesn't?

YOUR MOTIVATION

Fill in the blanks with information from your own birth chart.

Your Rising sign: _____

Your Rising sign element: _____

Your Rising sign modality: _____

Rising Sign Ruler

In the next chapter, we'll decode your Rising sign ruler's placement in your chart. Each sign has a ruling planet or luminary. Three signs (Pisces, Aquarius, and Scorpio) actually have two rulers—a traditional one and a modern one. For most of astrology's long history, astrologers only worked with the visible luminaries and planets (Sun, Moon, Mercury, Venus, Mars, Jupiter, and Saturn). The traditional ruler is the visible planet assigned to these three signs before Uranus, Neptune, and Pluto were discovered. For the purposes of decoding the placement of your Rising sign ruler, we'll only be considering the traditional ruler's placement. The reasoning behind this will be discussed in chapter 4, but for your reference, the traditional ruler of the sign will be listed in each entry in this chapter.

ARIES RISING

Motivated to . . .

INITIATE

DEFEND & CHAMPION

STRIKE OUT ALONE

PRIORITIZE SELF &
INDIVIDUALISM

As the cardinal fire sign, **ARIES** Rising is motivated by initiating action and leading the charge. Aries Rising hates to be idle: there's always a new inspiration to act on, a new activity to tackle. Generally, you know your own mind and are decisive—barring other factors that are prone to indecisiveness like a Libra Sun. This doesn't mean your plans are always well thought out or the right course of action, but rather that your drive to act may override your willingness to deliberate. You have a substantial amount of energy to start new projects, though whether you'll be able to see them through to the end depends on whether you have planets in earth or fixed signs to help you out.

Like the spear of Mars, sharp and pointed, you can be impressively direct, cutting through the front line, red tape, or a tedious conversation to get straight to the heart of the matter. You may feel particularly motivated to stand for something and have something to defend, especially standing up for yourself. Aries Rising is a fiercely independent energy. You value your agency and demand that others honor it as well. Aries Rising can be a great leader or entrepreneur because they don't require anyone else's validation to begin. That doesn't mean Aries is opposed to taking orders. Aries can be a good soldier as long as the general is someone you can respect. Your motivation may be more about the desire to take action than the desire to make decisions or strategize, so leaving that work up to a trusted leader could free you up from the tedium of the leadership and get you back to the action.

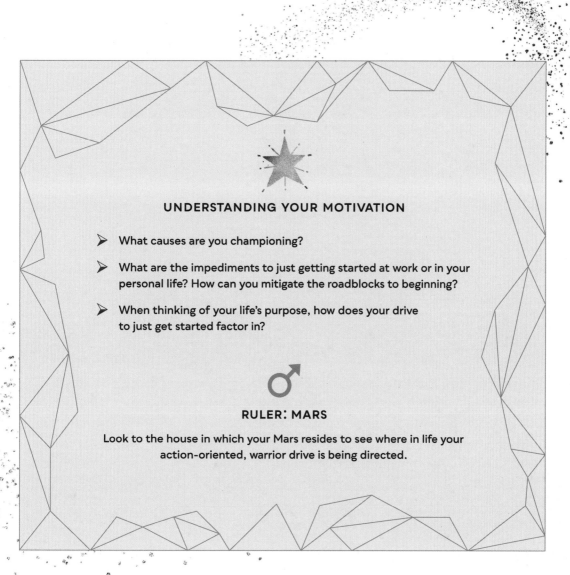

UNDERSTANDING YOUR MOTIVATION

➤ What causes are you championing?

➤ What are the impediments to just getting started at work or in your personal life? How can you mitigate the roadblocks to beginning?

➤ When thinking of your life's purpose, how does your drive to just get started factor in?

RULER: MARS

Look to the house in which your Mars resides to see where in life your action-oriented, warrior drive is being directed.

TAURUS RISING

Motivated to . . .

BUILD

GROW

LUXURIATE

BEAUTIFY

As the fixed earth sign, **TAURUS** rising is an energy of stabilization, persistence, and long-term growth. While ruled by Venus and delighting in the pleasures of the moment, Taurus also understands that anything worth doing is worth doing right, and that takes time. There is beauty and pleasure in each step of a project. You won't be rushed through any of it. With Taurus as your Rising sign, you may find it somewhat difficult to begin a new task, especially if it doesn't activate one of your core drives to build, stabilize, or beautify. There is an inertia to you, whether it is staying at rest or on a set path. Changing course or beginning might take significant force, but once in motion, you continue on with indefatigable commitment.

Ultimately, though, what motivates Taurus Rising most is enjoying pleasures, especially simple pleasures: good food, beautiful spaces, moving music, sumptuous textiles. You love your hobbies, getting your hands dirty, making something, or growing something.

Regardless of what pleasure you engage in, your key drive is to enjoy the process and persist. This doesn't always mean action. When cultivating the land for harvest, there are times of great activity (preparing the land, sowing the seeds, harvesting the crop), times of maintenance (tending to the growing crop), and times for rest and comfort (laying fallow in the winter). Understand that your motivation style, even as a fixed earth sign, doesn't mean interminable plodding and ceaseless production. Persistence doesn't mean the same level of effort continuously, but rather seeing things through and not giving up.

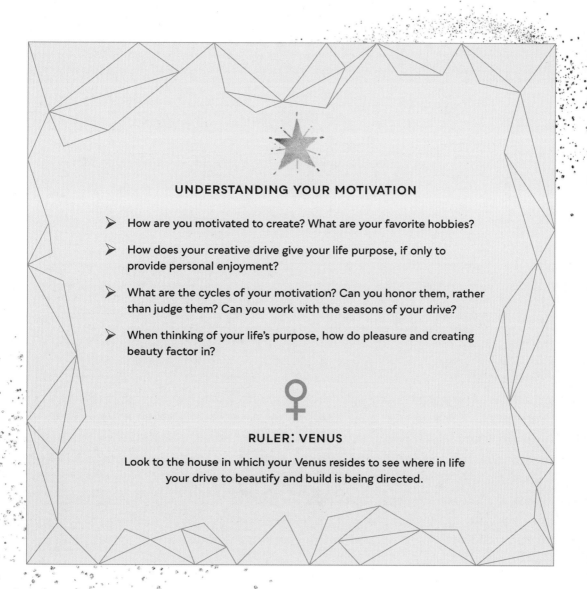

UNDERSTANDING YOUR MOTIVATION

➤ How are you motivated to create? What are your favorite hobbies?

➤ How does your creative drive give your life purpose, if only to provide personal enjoyment?

➤ What are the cycles of your motivation? Can you honor them, rather than judge them? Can you work with the seasons of your drive?

➤ When thinking of your life's purpose, how do pleasure and creating beauty factor in?

RULER: VENUS

Look to the house in which your Venus resides to see where in life your drive to beautify and build is being directed.

93

GEMINI RISING

Motivated to . . .

BE CURIOUS

INVESTIGATE

DISSEMINATE
KNOWLEDGE

Mutable signs abhor stagnation and perhaps none more than **GEMINI**. As an air sign, this aversion to monotony is particularly focused on intellectual pursuits. Gemini is an infinitely curious sign. With Gemini as your Rising sign, you are voracious for information and novelty. Every question begets another and you relish being able to investigate each new inquiry unbridled. Your brain is busy, excitable, and enthusiastic. Ruled by swift-footed Mercury, there is a speed to your thinking as your mind leaps from one stone to the next along your cerebral journey. This doesn't mean you're without the ability to focus or be diligent, especially if you have a number of placements in earth signs. Rather, having Gemini as your Rising sign means what motivates you is intellectual challenge, freedom, and variability.

In terms of work, the more intellectual variability and rigor you can muster, the better. It is unlikely, though, that your profession alone will scratch the itch of your inquisitive mind, so making time for hobbies and relationships that you find stimulating will be important for your happiness. You may find that you have a few domains of knowledge that are of particular interest and that are vast and complex enough to keep you coming back for more. A particular skill of Gemini is the ability to combine and synthesize disparate ideas. When considering the domains of knowledge that are most compelling to you, are there fresh combinations of them that could add something new to the world? One caution with Gemini rising is that the energy to think is always there and without engaging avenues to traverse, the mind can tend to overthink or turn to self-criticism.

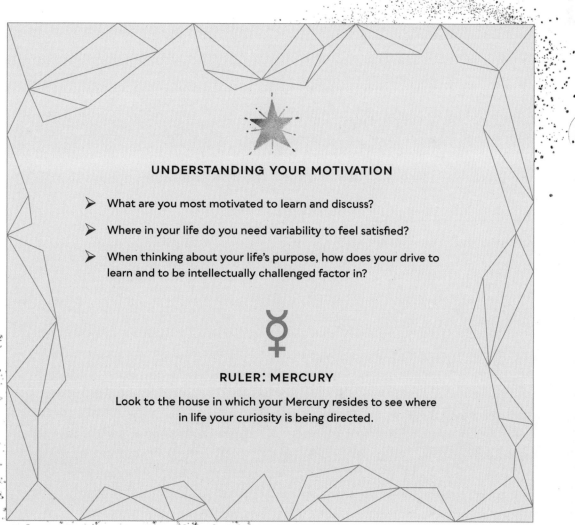

UNDERSTANDING YOUR MOTIVATION

➢ What are you most motivated to learn and discuss?

➢ Where in your life do you need variability to feel satisfied?

➢ When thinking about your life's purpose, how does your drive to learn and to be intellectually challenged factor in?

☿

RULER: MERCURY

Look to the house in which your Mercury resides to see where in life your curiosity is being directed.

CANCER RISING

Motivated to . . .

NURTURE

FOSTER COMMUNITY

FORGE MEANINGFUL
RELATIONSHIPS

With **CANCER** as your Rising sign, you are motivated by creating and caring for a close community. To you, your chosen people are family and you care for them with your impressive capacity for love. Being a Cancer Rising may motivate you to create many communities, a large community, or a small, intimate group. What motivates you is emotional intimacy and feeling connected to your chosen people. This desire to create meaningful relationships will manifest differently in personal versus professional contexts, but the underlying drive for connection and mutual care will be the through line of all you do.

Ruled by the Moon, Cancer is a gifted nurturer, intuiting the needs of others and being motivated to provide care and support to others. Caregiving is often maligned in Western culture, so you may recoil at this statement. Perhaps you've even had to stifle this aspect of your nature in order to conform to more socially valued traits. But in a world that is self-focused and self-serving, Cancer Rising's superpower is that they care. You can bring that care to any type of work and any relationship. In what relationships and what activities have you felt your ability to nurture was meaningful to you and valued by others? In what instances did you feel you gave too much or were taken for granted?

A difficulty for Cancer Rising folks is thinking that everyone approaches relationships with the same intuitive understanding and that they are committed to caregiving to the same degree and manner that you are. This can lead you to feeling that your relationships are unbalanced and that you are unappreciated. Working on boundaries that protect your energy so you don't give too much is essential, but so too is communicating your expectations of care to loved ones so that everyone is on the same page.

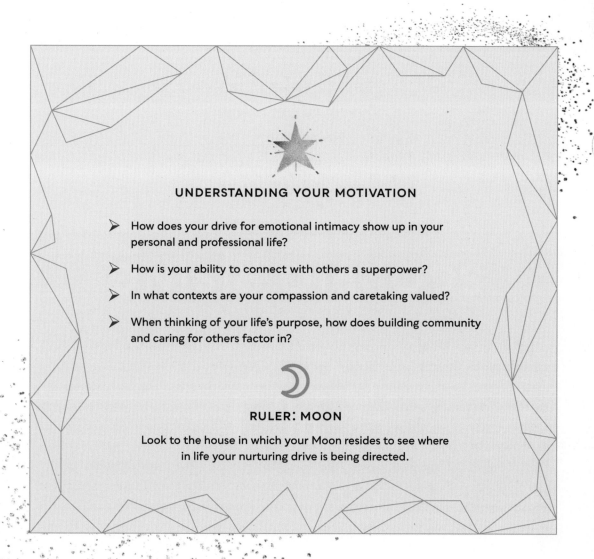

UNDERSTANDING YOUR MOTIVATION

➤ How does your drive for emotional intimacy show up in your personal and professional life?

➤ How is your ability to connect with others a superpower?

➤ In what contexts are your compassion and caretaking valued?

➤ When thinking of your life's purpose, how does building community and caring for others factor in?

RULER: MOON

Look to the house in which your Moon resides to see where in life your nurturing drive is being directed.

LEO RISING

Motivated to . . .

SHINE AUTHENTICALLY

ENTERTAIN

BE RECOGNIZED

Having **LEO** as your Rising sign means that you are motivated to perform and be recognized for that performance. Because Leo is ruled by the Sun, that means that your Sun sign and house are doubly important. Being recognized for however the Sun in your chart is calling you to express is what is most motivating to you. This doesn't mean you need a grand stage or that you're pandering for empty applause. You have something meaningful to share and you relish in recognition for that contribution.

A challenge of this placement is that while self-aggrandizement is seemingly ubiquitous in our social media age, there is also pervasive judgment of those with the audacity to take up space and claim the limelight, especially for those in groups previously disenfranchised from mainstream culture. Just because you feel motivated by recognition for how your Sun shines doesn't mean you haven't internalized societal shaming of that drive. These warring emotions can leave you conflicted and unfulfilled.

In considering your Sun sign and house (part I), when have you felt most in flow and most energized in front of others? What is your performance of choice? What recognition matters to you and from whom? It is possible with this placement to be too reliant on the praise of others for your sense of identity. You may also be too boastful and full of yourself. But in my experience, most individuals struggle with self-doubt, the pressure to be self-effacing and small, and the fear of ridicule or rejection. That's not what you're here for in this life. You are here to shine. You are here to be bold, generous, and magnanimous. You are here to take up space and you will find your audience when you shine your beautiful, unique light.

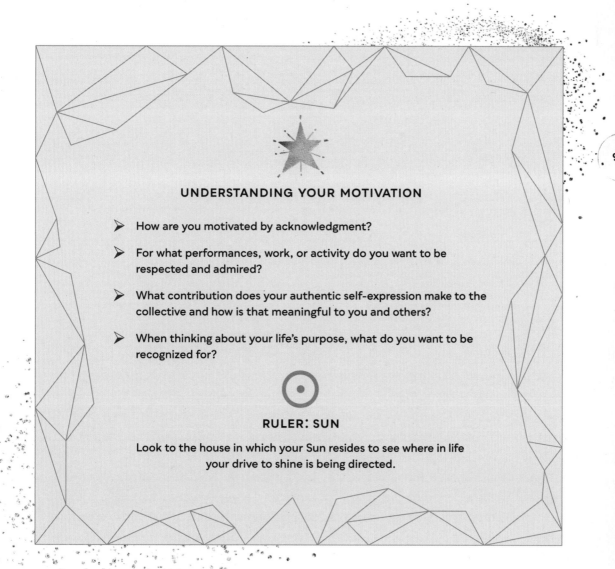

UNDERSTANDING YOUR MOTIVATION

➤ How are you motivated by acknowledgment?

➤ For what performances, work, or activity do you want to be respected and admired?

➤ What contribution does your authentic self-expression make to the collective and how is that meaningful to you and others?

➤ When thinking about your life's purpose, what do you want to be recognized for?

RULER: SUN

Look to the house in which your Sun resides to see where in life your drive to shine is being directed.

VIRGO RISING

Motivated to . . .

DISCERN

PERFECT

REFINE & EDIT

With **VIRGO** as your Rising sign, your primary motivation is to improve and perfect. Ruled by Mercury, the planet that represents mental acuity and communication, you are motivated to understand, to parse out, to evaluate, to judge. You use your impressive abilities of discernment to assess any situation and devise the best course of action. You create spreadsheets. You make the task list. You want to understand. Every bit of information belongs in its place and should fit into your schema. You are motivated to make things make sense.

While Gemini—your fellow Mercury-ruled sign—is about the proliferation of ideas, you are about the evaluation and sorting of ideas. Your earthy nature seeks tangible, identifiable results for all the mental gymnastics you engage in. You're still motivated by mutable energy, so you aren't as intractable as the other earth signs might be. You aren't satisfied with things as they are. You are constantly pushing for change. You can't be content with admiring a problem. You're looking for resolution, clarity, and correctness.

Virgo is also a sign of service, so you may feel a strong drive to use your problem-solving powers to help others. This may be through a healing modality, like the medical profession or psychology. You want your work to mean something. You don't care about perfection for perfection's sake alone, so employing your skills to improve the lives of others is particularly gratifying.

A challenge of Virgo Rising is that you might not know when to stop. Everything can be improved. There's always another task to complete. Every thought, argument, or plan can be reevaluated. When you run out of things to dissect, you can end up turning your perfecting gaze on yourself or loved ones, looking for problems where there aren't any. Developing ways to quiet the mind, perhaps through exercise or mindfulness, would be time well spent.

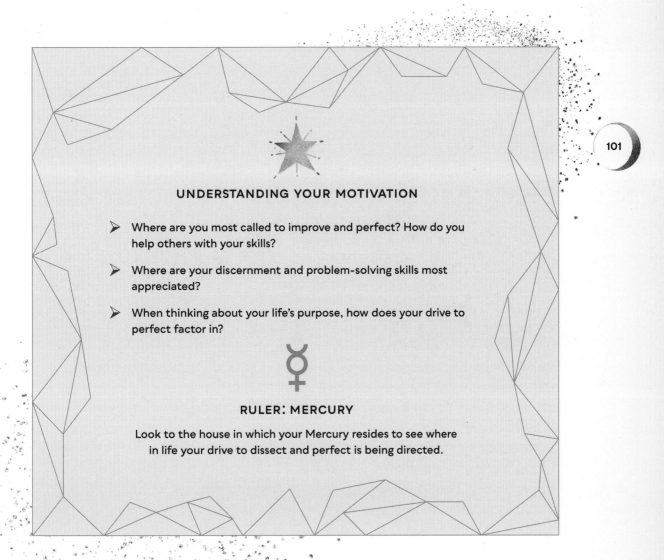

UNDERSTANDING YOUR MOTIVATION

➤ Where are you most called to improve and perfect? How do you help others with your skills?

➤ Where are your discernment and problem-solving skills most appreciated?

➤ When thinking about your life's purpose, how does your drive to perfect factor in?

RULER: MERCURY

Look to the house in which your Mercury resides to see where in life your drive to dissect and perfect is being directed.

LIBRA RISING

Motivated to . . .

BALANCE

MEDIATE

ADVOCATE FOR JUSTICE

CULTIVATE BEAUTY

Your **LIBRA** Rising motivates you to create balance in all aspects of life: equitable relationships, symmetry in interior design, peace among friends. Ruled by Venus—goddess of love, beauty, and art—you are motivated by a deep desire for harmony. As a cardinal sign, you are blessed with initiative to start new endeavors and take charge. As an air sign, your domain is more cerebral than your fellow Venus-ruled sign, earthy Taurus. Whereas Taurus is interested in the sensual, valuing the materiality and experience of beauty, Libra is interested in the aesthetic judgment of art and all the trappings of cultural expression and exchange. Libra enjoys making and enjoying beauty, sure, but Libra excels at the intellectual endeavor of the intersection of culture, history, and art. Your Libra Rising compels you to be cultured, informed, and worldly.

Libran balance also manifests as the drive for justice and equality, which influences you in ways great and small. For instance, you appreciate when people follow social niceties. The rules matter to you because, from your perspective, adherence to the rules creates peace and protects others from mistreatment. Avoiding social discord is a major motivator for you. But your drive for justice may encompass your community or perhaps the whole world. You may feel called to use your brilliant mind to strive for global climate justice or advocate for marginalized communities.

The main question for you, in terms of your life's purpose, is what harmony is most important to you? What balance do you most want to influence in the world? It may be that you want to create harmony as a musician in an orchestra, or as a mediator, or perhaps as a writer drawing attention to widening economic disparities and advocating for increased governmental regulations. For you, harmony is everything in its appropriate proportion—be that artistically, intellectually, or legally. What is equitable, fair, and right?

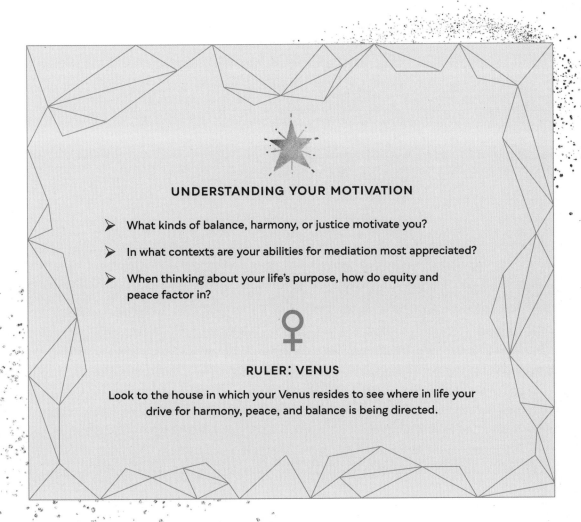

UNDERSTANDING YOUR MOTIVATION

➤ What kinds of balance, harmony, or justice motivate you?

➤ In what contexts are your abilities for mediation most appreciated?

➤ When thinking about your life's purpose, how do equity and peace factor in?

RULER: VENUS

Look to the house in which your Venus resides to see where in life your drive for harmony, peace, and balance is being directed.

SCORPIO RISING

Motivated to . . .

UNCOVER THE TRUTH

FACILITATE
TRANSFORMATION

CALL ATTENTION TO
WHAT IS TABOO

With the power and tenacity of Mars, **SCORPIO** Rising is motivated to cut to the heart of the matter. Shovel in hand, you're ready to dig up the bodies and lay everything out to be scrutinized. No topic is too taboo for you—the more uncomfortable, the better. You know that nothing meaningful ever happens and nothing ever changes until we drop the facades and the niceties and get real.

Scorpio is the sign that deals with death, transformation, and rebirth. You understand that everything ends and from those ashes, something new can begin. You crave the revelatory power of the Underworld journey, for yourself or as a guide for others. You ferry them across the river Styx, walk them into the very heart of hell, and then back out again. Where in your life do you wade into the muck—for yourself or others? How do you employ this superpower of having hard conversations and sitting with discomfort? How do you facilitate the ending of one thing and the birth of something new?

Your fixed nature is not one of stagnation or stubbornness, but rather an ability to hold the center during the tumultuous upheaval that is destruction and renewal. You can create a container for others in which they might dissolve and reassemble their parts. Your capacity for deep emotional intimacy is unique and powerful. How will you use your powers for good?

All of this might sound very intense, because it is. Scorpio has emotional and intellectual depth and intensity. But that doesn't mean that you show this to many people. It may simmer beneath your Scorpionic exoskeleton, especially if your Sun is placed in a more staid sign like Taurus, Virgo, Capricorn, Libra, or Aquarius. Your ability to facilitate change doesn't have to be ostentatious. The key motivation of Scorpio Rising is the drive for truth, to peel back the layers until the core is found, to see what lies beneath. This can be done in a library, on an archeological site, sitting in meditation, talking with a friend, brokering a business deal. Where do you feel called to push forward?

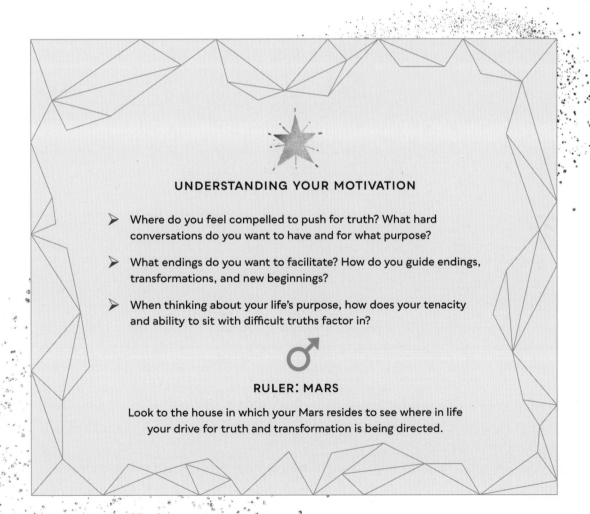

UNDERSTANDING YOUR MOTIVATION

➤ Where do you feel compelled to push for truth? What hard conversations do you want to have and for what purpose?

➤ What endings do you want to facilitate? How do you guide endings, transformations, and new beginnings?

➤ When thinking about your life's purpose, how does your tenacity and ability to sit with difficult truths factor in?

RULER: MARS

Look to the house in which your Mars resides to see where in life your drive for truth and transformation is being directed.

SAGITTARIUS RISING

Motivated to . . .

**SEEK, EXPERIENCE
& LEARN**

LIVE OPTIMISTICALLY

**TAKE A LEAP
OF FAITH**

With **SAGITTARIUS** as your Rising sign, you are motivated by an optimistic, adventurous spirit to seek out new experiences and knowledge. As a mutable sign, you are, in part, driven by the joy of novelty and the thrill of the unknown. But also core to your nature is an inexorable pull to seek the Truth, with a capital T. One of the facets of Jupiter, Sagittarius's ruling planet, is the archetype of the philosopher. Part of your nature is that intellectual and spiritual desire to ask the big questions. Who am I? Why are we here? What does it all mean? What is love? Who is God? It is through your intrepid traveling that you appease both your unquenchable call to adventure and your drive to experience ineffable truth.

Spirituality will likely be alluring. In your search for truth, you'll be called to seek out various wisdom traditions and belief systems. Your spiritual journey is unlikely to favor rigid religious systems. Instead, you believe that there is truth to be learned from every discipline and faith. You are open-minded and interested in experiencing the subjective truths of different peoples in different contexts to uncover the underlying, deeper wisdom that connects them all.

Like all fire signs, you are driven by passion, demand freedom, and are fulfilled through experience. You likely will loathe sitting, waiting, debating, or revising. You are ready to go out and do. Embracing your fiery nature and finding ways to reduce roadblocks to action and adventure will help you feel more in flow.

If you have several planets placed in air signs or if Jupiter is placed in the 3rd or 9th House, you may find that intellectual adventures are more interesting to you than physical expeditions, though experiential learning will likely always be a major component of your life.

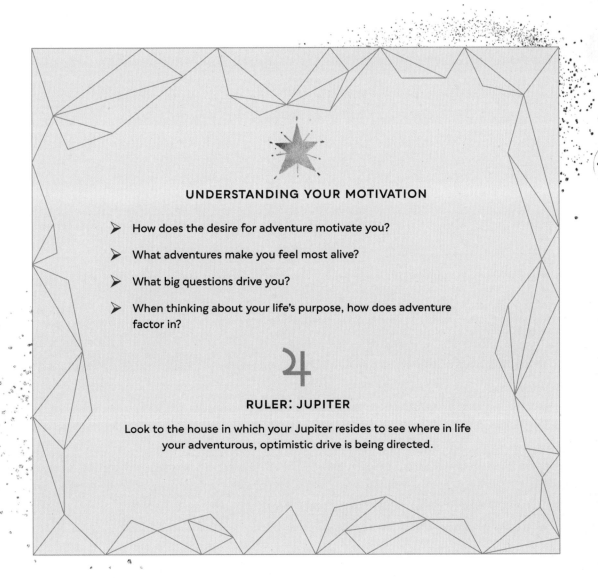

UNDERSTANDING YOUR MOTIVATION

➤ How does the desire for adventure motivate you?

➤ What adventures make you feel most alive?

➤ What big questions drive you?

➤ When thinking about your life's purpose, how does adventure factor in?

♃

RULER: JUPITER

Look to the house in which your Jupiter resides to see where in life your adventurous, optimistic drive is being directed.

CAPRICORN RISING

Motivated to . . .

ACHIEVE

LEAD

PERSIST

With **CAPRICORN** as your Rising sign, you are motivated by achievement. You set goals and you work tirelessly to accomplish them. Like Capricorn's ruling planet, Saturn, you value structure, organization, and responsibility. You feel least in flow without clear metrics for success. Whether personally or professionally, you appreciate having the rules of engagement spelled out and having a detailed map to the finish line. Unless you have several planets in mutable signs, you will likely abhor work where much of your job description is "to be determined" or "other responsibilities as assigned." The more you're able to define goals in your personal and professional life—and have the resources and wherewithal to achieve them—the better you'll feel.

As a cardinal sign, your Capricorn Rising makes you eager to initiate and lead new projects that have tangible outcomes. Due to the earthy nature of your Rising sign, you are motivated to engage in the material world and to accrue material security. While other planetary placements in your chart may call you to a life of the mind (air), to relationships (water), or to action and passion (fire), your Capricorn Rising firmly roots your life's purpose in the measurable and substantial world.

You are not afraid of responsibility, self-denial, and hard work in service of your goal. Persistence is your middle name. This isn't to say that you don't enjoy philosophy or relaxing, but rather that you feel most inspired and are fulfilled when you set a task and accomplish it. The bigger the goal, the better. There is an aspect of Capricorn that appreciates recognition. Not in the Leo sense of applause, necessarily, but more specifically acknowledgment that you've attained your goal. As an earth sign focused on the material world, the goals you define may fall into more traditional ideas of success (degrees, promotions, buying a house, etc.).

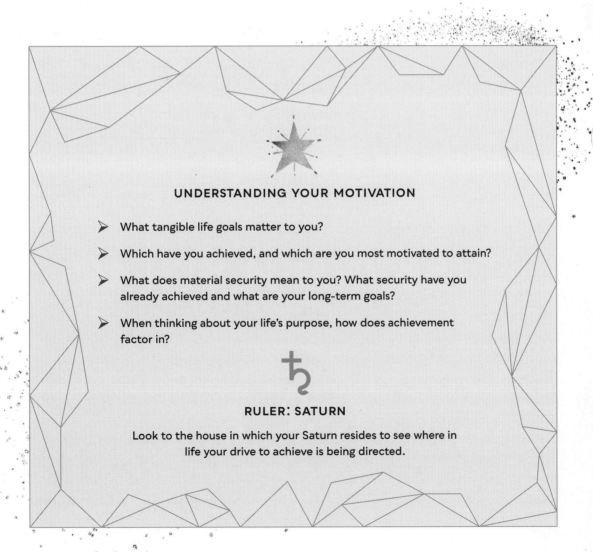

UNDERSTANDING YOUR MOTIVATION

➤ What tangible life goals matter to you?

➤ Which have you achieved, and which are you most motivated to attain?

➤ What does material security mean to you? What security have you already achieved and what are your long-term goals?

➤ When thinking about your life's purpose, how does achievement factor in?

♄

RULER: SATURN

Look to the house in which your Saturn resides to see where in life your drive to achieve is being directed.

AQUARIUS RISING

Motivated to . . .

**UNDERSTAND THE
BIG PICTURE**

**TAKE A UNIQUE
APPROACH**

**INFLUENCE THE
COLLECTIVE**

With **AQUARIUS** as your Rising sign, you are motivated by understanding the larger picture and coming up with unique solutions. You have a gift for disentangling emotions that might muddy the waters, allowing you to formulate conclusions dispassionately. You prefer to bring a calm, clear eye to a situation and, in true Saturnian fashion, develop a methodical solution. You are a systems thinker, a strategist, and an innovator.

Finding the kinds of problems you most like to solve will be key to determining your life's purpose. Think back to times when you had to solve complex problems. When did you feel in flow? What felt good and supportive during those instances? What felt stifling? Who do you most want to help with your problem-solving capabilities? There is a community-minded aspect of Aquarius that could motivate you to act in service of a larger group or humanity as a whole.

So much of what exists remains because of inertia. Unseating outmoded ways of thinking and behaving seems impossible, and yet Aquarius is uniquely suited to identify and uproot that which is obsolete. You innately bristle at maintaining inefficient systems for tradition's sake. What revolutions do you want to start? What antiquated systems do you want to tear down?

Aquarius seeks freedom and agency. There is something of a rebel or an outsider to Aquarius. In addition to railing against archaic customs on a systems level, your drive for rebellion may be more personal. You may choose your own path, irrespective of the expectations of your family or society. This could mean having a unique appearance, career path, or identity that falls outside of what is deemed traditional by societal standards. Consider how being true to your uniqueness motivates your life choices, actions, and sense of purpose.

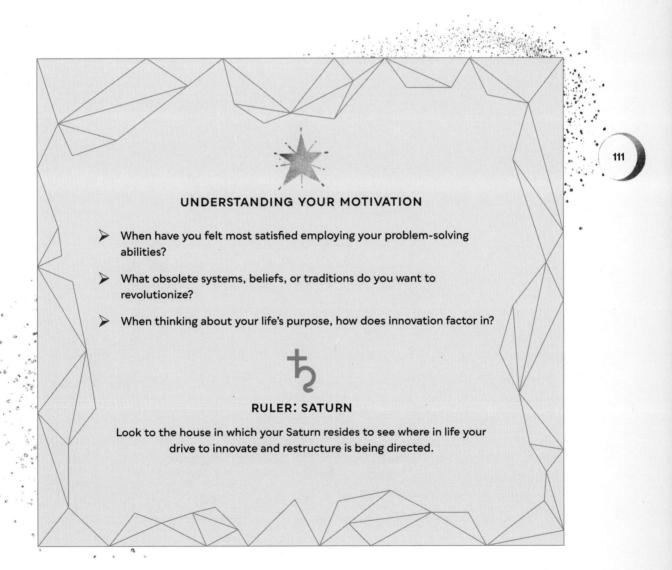

111

UNDERSTANDING YOUR MOTIVATION

➤ When have you felt most satisfied employing your problem-solving abilities?

➤ What obsolete systems, beliefs, or traditions do you want to revolutionize?

➤ When thinking about your life's purpose, how does innovation factor in?

♄

RULER: SATURN

Look to the house in which your Saturn resides to see where in life your drive to innovate and restructure is being directed.

PISCES RISING

Motivated to . . .

CONNECT

DISSOLVE BOUNDARIES

KNOW &
COMMUNICATE
DIVINE TRUTH

With **PISCES** as your Rising sign, you are motivated by a desire to feel connected and allow others to feel universal connection. Pisces energy is that of Divine Oneness. Pisces is about dissolution of self to realize the truth that separation is an illusion and we are all always connected. This oneness can be experienced any number of ways: through meditation, music, art, love, or nature. Pisces, more than any other sign, experiences and seeks this experience. There is beauty and wisdom to be found here and you are motivated to achieve this experience of connectedness or to foster it for others. You are as likely to be a poet as a priestess.

Look to where Jupiter resides in your chart to see where this transcendental drive is steering you. Jupiter is the traditional ruling planet of Pisces and imbues you with a powerful faith. Where you place that faith is up to you. Jupiter is the archetypal philosopher, teacher, and sage. A wisdom seeker, Jupiter motivates you to learn the truths of the universe through study and experience, and perhaps also to share that wisdom with others.

Consider the times that felt most transcendent. When have you felt most connected? What situations facilitated that feeling of connection? Do you feel called to help others access faith and spirituality? Pisces wants us to forgo, if only for a moment, the identities and ideologies we've constructed to separate us and see the truth of our interdependence and connection. How does this play a motivating role in your life?

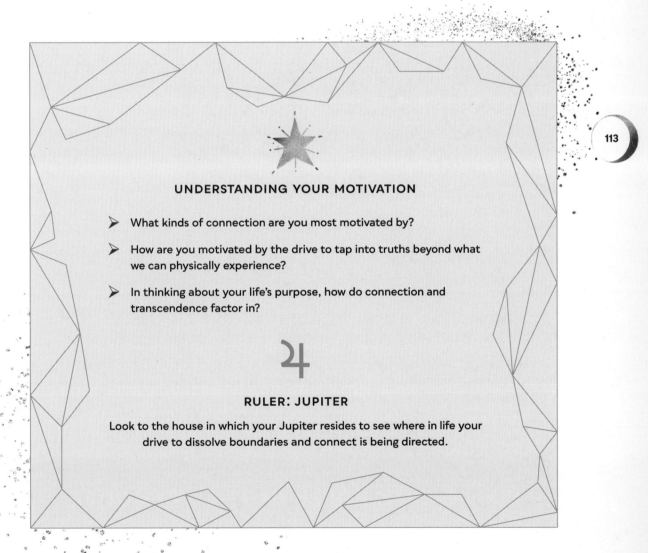

UNDERSTANDING YOUR MOTIVATION

➤ What kinds of connection are you most motivated by?

➤ How are you motivated by the drive to tap into truths beyond what we can physically experience?

➤ In thinking about your life's purpose, how do connection and transcendence factor in?

♃

RULER: JUPITER

Look to the house in which your Jupiter resides to see where in life your drive to dissolve boundaries and connect is being directed.

Your Rising Sign Ruler

WHERE YOU ARE STEERED

YOUR RISING SIGN describes what motivates you in life. What drives you. Ancient astrologers referred to the Rising sign as the helm of the ship, that is, the place from which the ship is steered. But where are you being steered? In this nautical metaphor, what steers the ship of your life is your Rising sign's ruling luminary or planet. Recall from **Understanding the Code** that every zodiacal sign has a luminary or planet that rules it (e.g., Aries is ruled by Mars). The house placement of your Rising sign ruler is where the ship of your life is being steered. In this chapter, we'll decode the house placement of your Rising sign ruler and how it factors into your life's purpose.

Your Rising Sign's Traditional Ruler

For millennia, astrologers only had the seven visible luminaries and planets (Sun, Moon, Mercury, Venus, Mars, Jupiter, and Saturn) to consider. These seven celestial bodies were each assigned as rulers to the twelve zodiacal signs (see Traditional Rulership chart). As more planets were discovered, astrologers assigned them each one zodiacal sign to rule. As a result, three signs (Aquarius, Pisces, and Scorpio) have two rulers: a traditional and a modern one.

For the purposes of this chapter and decoding the meaning of the Rising sign ruler's house placement, I encourage you to only consider the traditional ruler and not the modern one. The modern planets (Uranus, Neptune, and Pluto) move much more slowly than the traditional planets. Because it takes them so much longer to trek through each zodiacal sign, their significance is more generational than it is personal.

There are many astrologers who would disagree with this approach, however. So, if you have Aquarius, Pisces, or Scorpio Rising, and you feel so called, you can read the house description for your modern ruler as well. As always, take what resonates and leave what doesn't.

TRADITIONAL RULERSHIP

SIGN	TRADITIONAL RULER
Aries	Mars
Taurus	Venus
Gemini	Mercury
Cancer	Moon
Leo	Sun
Virgo	Mercury
Libra	Venus
Scorpio	Mars
Sagittarius	Jupiter
Capricorn	Saturn
Aquarius	Saturn
Pisces	Jupiter

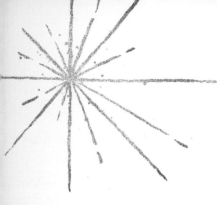

MODERN RULERSHIP

PLANET	DISCOVERED	RULES
Uranus	1781	Aquarius
Neptune	1846	Pisces
Pluto	1930	Scorpio

PLANETARY SPEED

PLANETS	1 YEAR*	AVERAGE TIME SPENT TRANSITING A ZODIACAL SIGN *±
Mercury	88 days	14 days
Venus	225 days	4.5 weeks
Mars	687 days	6.5 weeks
Jupiter	12 years	1 year
Saturn	30 years	2.5 years
Uranus	84 years	7 years
Neptune	165 years	14 years
Pluto	248 years	14 to 30 years

* In Earth days, weeks, or years.
± A planet will spend longer in a sign during a retrograde.

The Big Three

Your Sun, Rising, and Moon placements are the major three elements of your chart, describing your most fundamental nature and purpose. Your Sun house, Rising sign ruler's house, and Moon house taken together describe the most important areas of life for you. Where and how you live out your life's purpose will be a blend of the meanings of these three houses. If your Rising sign ruler is either the Sun (for Leo Rising folks) or the Moon (for Cancer Rising folks), then there is additional emphasis put on the topics of your Sun or Moon house, respectively.

Read through the description of your Rising sign ruler's house, then check out the **Cracking the Code: Your Motivation** section to reflect on how your Rising sign and its ruler help unpack your life's purpose.

WHERE YOUR LIFE IS STEERED

Fill in the blanks with information from your own birth chart.

Your Rising sign: _____

Your Rising sign's traditional ruler: _____

Your Rising sign ruler's house: _____

YOUR RISING SIGN RULER

RISING SIGN RULER IN THE 1st HOUSE

STEERED TOWARD SELF
AND IDENTITY

The Rising sign always contains the **1st HOUSE**, so to have your Rising sign ruler in the 1st House means that it is in its home sign. For example, if you are a Virgo Rising, and have Mercury in Virgo in the 1st House, then the ruler of your Rising sign is in its home sign. This placement imbues your Rising sign ruler with added power and the resources it needs to fully express.

The 1st House is the house of self and identity. To have your Rising sign ruler placed here means that your life is steered in the direction of yourself and your personal journey—sharing your story, focusing on personal growth, following your own path, striving for your dreams. Your Rising sign (chapter 3) will give you information about the style of self-inquiry and expression you're being steered toward.

Perhaps you feel affirmed knowing that your life direction is about developing yourself, but for many it may feel uncomfortable claiming this aspect of your chart. There can be societal pressure to prioritize others and be self-effacing. If you feel an aversion to this placement, get curious about that reaction. What narratives and values have you internalized from society about taking up space and prioritizing yourself? How can you find a way to let go of any internalized shame around prioritizing yourself?

Other aspects of your chart may seem to conflict with this placement. For example, if your Sun is in the 7th House, you may feel most energized when being in committed partnerships and working in collaboration. What you have to realize is that to have your life steered toward self-expression and development is not at odds with caring about or being in relationships with others.

DECODING YOUR RISING SIGN RULER'S HOUSE

➤ In what ways are you called to prioritize your personal development?

➤ How is claiming your unique, authentic identity central to your life's journey?

➤ In thinking about your life's purpose, how is it steered toward self-expression?

RISING SIGN RULER IN THE 2ND HOUSE

STEERED TOWARD MONEY, ASSETS, AND SKILLS

The **2ND HOUSE** is the place of your money and assets, the skills with which you make money, and how you manage your finances. When the Rising sign ruler is located here, your life is being steered toward the management or making of money. Your life may be steered toward working in the financial sector, but more generally this placement indicates that your life's purpose will be lived out through your work. See part IV of this book for more information on your 2nd House, including discussion of the skills with which you make money and how they support the development of your career.

More than just the importance of your work, having your Rising sign ruler in the 2nd House speaks to the importance of financial independence in your life. Your relationship to personal finance and financial autonomy will be a central theme in your life. What is your relationship with money? What are the stories that you have internalized around money? Developing a positive relationship with your work and money could prove to be a transformative and empowering journey for you.

119

DECODING YOUR RISING SIGN RULER'S HOUSE

➤ What is the role of personal finance, monetary stability, and financial independence in your life?

➤ Do you feel that achieving financial independence is a critical component of living a fulfilling life?

➤ How does your life's motivation, described by your Rising sign (chapter 3), drive you toward your work and financial autonomy?

STEERED TOWARD COMMUNICATION, LOCAL COMMUNITY, AND SIBLINGS

The **3RD HOUSE** is the place of communication. However your Sun sign calls you to shine, and however your Rising sign motivates you, you're being steered toward communicating. Communication comes in many forms. This could be as a teacher, writer, dancer, actor, podcaster, salesperson, or activist. Look to the sign of your 3rd House for information about how you're called to communicate. Your Sun sign (chapter 1) and house (chapter 2) give clues as to the topics you're interested in communicating about. Balancing all of these aspects, think about when you've felt most in flow communicating. Were you alone painting or talking before a packed auditorium? What were you communicating? What were its contents and purpose? What are you most passionate about sharing?

The 3rd House is also the house of siblings, your local area, and education (especially elementary and secondary education), so you may find yourself pulled toward these arenas in living out your life's purpose. Perhaps collaborating with or having strong bonds with your siblings, being active in your local community, or working in education will be main features of your life.

120

DECODING YOUR RISING SIGN RULER'S HOUSE

➤ What messages do you want to communicate? What knowledge do you want to teach?

➤ What conversations do you want to have?

➤ What audiences do you want to connect with?

➤ How does your life's motivation, described by your Rising sign (chapter 3), drive you to communicate?

STEERED TOWARD HOME,
FAMILY, AND LINEAGE

The **4TH HOUSE** is the place of home, family, and lineage. To have your Rising sign ruler here steers your life toward the concerns of home. This may be expressed in your life as the desire to build a home and family.

Whatever the pull toward home and whatever the type of home and family you wish to create, your life's purpose is concerned with this foundational place. This doesn't mean that you don't have a career or enjoy doing things outside of the home—though it may mean that you prefer to work from home. Rather, this placement denotes that issues of home and family are an essential component of your life's purpose. It may be that you are steered toward issues of the home in a less personal sense, perhaps as a social worker working with families or as an interior designer beautifying the homes of others.

The 4th House is also the place of our ancestors and ties to our personal lineage. You may feel called to research your family's past or aid others in discovering their history or healing ancestral wounds. This placement could call you to write novels set in your ancestral homeland, or alternatively to fight for justice for the wrongs done to your ancestors.

DECODING YOUR RISING SIGN RULER'S HOUSE

➢ What role do home and family play in the life you want to build?

➢ What is your relationship to your lineage? How do your ancestors and all you've inherited from them inform your sense of purpose?

➢ How does your life's motivation, described by your Rising sign (chapter 3), connect with issues of home, family, and ancestors?

RISING SIGN RULER IN THE 5TH HOUSE

STEERED TOWARD CREATIVITY
AND CHILDREN

The **5TH HOUSE** is the place of creative energy in your chart. It is where your intellectual, artistic, and physical offspring are conceived, cultivated, and birthed. To have your Rising sign ruler here means your life is steered toward your creative work, to your relationship with your own children, or to caring for and working with children more generally.

The 5th House is also more generally the house of pleasure and fun. Sometimes that pleasure is part of a creative act, but the 5th House is also concerned with the creation of pleasure as an end unto itself. You may find that your life is steered toward pursuits of pleasure or creating pleasurable experiences for others. Balance this placement with the topics of your Sun's house to get a fuller picture of how creativity, pleasure, and/or children are essential to your life's purpose.

DECODING YOUR RISING SIGN RULER'S HOUSE

➤ What role does creativity play in your life?

➤ How do children factor into your life's purpose? Do you have (or want to have) your own children? Do you want to work with children?

➤ How do your creative works give meaning and purpose to your life?

STEERED TOWARD DAILY WORK,
HABITS, AND HEALTH

The **6TH HOUSE** is the place of your day-to-day work and the daily schedules and habits that facilitate your daily work. It is also the place of our personal health, which to a large extent is the product of our daily habits. To have your Rising sign ruler here means that your life is steered toward your daily life. Your life's purpose requires you to cultivate your daily habits and rituals. (See part IV for more information about your 6th House and your work.)

A gift of this placement is that your motivation supports your daily work and, ultimately, if you want to accomplish anything, you have to take it one day at a time and one task at a time. But just because your Rising sign ruler is here doesn't mean that you have your daily schedule honed so that it is productive and supportive. What this placement encourages you to do is focus on your day-to-day life and your physical well-being, creating the habits necessary to live the life that you want to live and accomplish your goals.

123

DECODING YOUR RISING SIGN RULER'S HOUSE

➤ What are your daily rituals, schedules, and work like? Are they chaotic, or have you cultivated them to support your larger life goals?

➤ What habits have you established to maintain your health and what role does your physical health play in your life's purpose?

➤ How does your life's motivation, described by your Rising sign (chapter 3), drive you to focus on your daily habits and work?

STEERED TOWARD COLLABORATION
AND COMMITTED PARTNERSHIP

The **7TH HOUSE** is the place of committed partnership (romantic, platonic, and business). To have your Rising sign ruler here indicates that your life is steered toward partnership. Living out your life's purpose will be a collaborative affair and likely the result of many different kinds of partnership.

The relationships under the purview of this house are primarily between two people where the participants have established obligations to one another, either tacitly agreed upon (as with longtime friends who have developed understood roles over time) or contractually agreed upon (as in marriage or business partnerships). You likely feel called toward meaningful partnership in your personal and professional life. Being in partnership, in and of itself, isn't your life's purpose, but collaborations will feature prominently in how you live out your life's purpose. This placement could indicate that you find fulfillment working as a marriage and family therapist, agent, mediator, coach, or some other collaborative professional. Alternatively, committed friendships or a romantic partnership may be central to living out your purpose.

DECODING YOUR RISING SIGN RULER'S HOUSE

➤ What have been the major partnerships in your life and how have they contributed to your understanding of your life's purpose?

➤ How does partnership help support the way you shine, described by your Sun sign (chapter 1)?

➤ How does your life's motivation, described by your Rising sign (chapter 3), drive you to focus on your committed partnerships?

STEERED TOWARD SHARED RESOURCES, ENDINGS, AND TRANSFORMATION

The **8TH HOUSE** is a complex, multifaceted place in the birth chart. It has many significations and only some of them are likely to resonate with you. The 8th House is the place of shared assets and resources, other people's money, and the money we owe others and what they owe us (e.g., loans, taxes, and joint accounts fall under the purview of the 8th House). Having your Rising sign ruler placed here could indicate that you are steered toward the management of other people's resources. I've read for literary agents and art gallery curators who had prominent 8th House placements, and they lived out that energy through the curation and management of other people's intellectual property.

But there is much more to this house. It is also the place of death, transformation, and rebirth. As such, you may feel called to engage with this cycle as a hospice nurse, but equally as plausible is being drawn to composting and gardening, or perhaps a career advisor helping people through the end of one career path and the beginning of another. There are innumerable endings and beginnings in our lives and the 8th House reminds us of that.

This house is also the place of grief and mental illness. If this aspect resonates with you, you may feel steered toward the mental health field or mental health might be an important facet of your life's purpose. It's rare that anyone engages with all elements of the 8th House in equal measure, so it's likely that you'll immediately resonate with one aspect of this house. Trust your intuition and remember that this is just one element of the larger tapestry of your birth chart and the code of your life's purpose.

125

DECODING YOUR RISING SIGN RULER'S HOUSE

➤ What role, if any, does managing other people's assets play in your life?

➤ How do endings, transformations, and new beginnings feature in your life and work?

➤ How does your life's motivation, described by your Rising sign (chapter 3), drive you to engage with the topics of the 8th House?

STEERED TOWARD LEARNING, TEACHING, SPIRITUALITY, AND TRAVEL

———

The **9TH HOUSE** is the place of higher learning, teaching, publishing, and long-distance travel. With your Rising sign ruler here, you're driven toward learning and sharing what you know. You feel a call to seek. With this placement, your life's purpose may take you far and wide, or perhaps just deep into the library, but the impetus is the same: to learn. This is also a placement that denotes teaching, writing, publishing, and speaking and the general dissemination of your wisdom. What do you want to share with the world? How has your life been directed toward learning and teaching? What do you feel called to research?

The 9th House is also the place of spirituality and belief systems. It is about the study of the Divine (whereas the 12th House may more rightly be the place where we *experience* the Divine). How has your life been steered toward spiritual practice and study? Have you felt called to be a teacher on spiritual topics? How does this blend with the significations of your Sun sign and house?

DECODING YOUR RISING SIGN RULER'S HOUSE

➤ What do you feel called to learn?

➤ What role does learning play in giving your life meaning?

➤ What do you feel called to teach or share? How do you feel called to share (e.g., writing, speaking, performing)?

➤ What role does spirituality play in giving your life meaning?

➤ How does your life's motivation, described by your Rising sign (chapter 3), drive you toward learning, traveling, teaching, or publishing?

STEERED TOWARD CAREER
AND PUBLIC LIFE

The **10TH HOUSE** is the highest point in your birth chart, and like the noonday Sun, it's where you shine most visibly. It is the place in the chart dealing with your public life and what you do to attain notoriety and acclaim. It is also the place of your career, which we could think of as the curated collection of all your public work. With the Rising sign ruler here, you are steered toward living out your life's purpose via your career. Whereas the 6th House is the actual day-to-day work you complete, the 10th House is the overarching story of your collective professional endeavors. What do you want to accomplish in your career? How do you wish to distinguish yourself in the world? What acclaim do you seek? What is the legacy you want to leave? See part IV for more information on the 10th House and other aspects of your chart that speak to your professional life.

127

DECODING YOUR RISING SIGN RULER'S HOUSE

➢ How does your career give your life meaning and purpose?

➢ What do you want to be known for? What legacy do you want to create?

➢ How does your life's motivation, described by your Rising sign (chapter 3), drive you in your career?

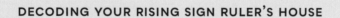

STEERED TOWARD COMMUNITIES, FRIENDS, AND PATRONS

The **11TH HOUSE** is the place of community in the chart. It is about groups of people—from personal friend groups, to fan groups, to nations, to the entire human collective. With your Rising sign ruler here, your life is steered toward engaging with or building community. This placement often relates to creating a following, as a celebrity, a community organizer, or a politician, or in a career that requires building a clientele.

What communities are you drawn to? Are you a trailblazer or a facilitator? What motivates you to build community (your Rising sign)? While it is likely that this placement would result in a public life—gathering people together and establishing a following—it is entirely possible that you build a community and not live life in the public eye. The Internet creates opportunities for connection and community building without the need for in-person socialization, so if you identify as a more introverted person, know that this placement doesn't require extreme extroversion.

DECODING YOUR RISING SIGN RULER'S HOUSE

➤ What communities are most important to you? Which give your life meaning?

➤ How do the communities you build allow you to shine in the style of your Sun sign (chapter 1)?

➤ How does your life's motivation, described by your Rising sign (chapter 3), drive you to engage with or create community?

STEERED TOWARD HIDDEN LIFE, THE UNCONSCIOUS MIND, AND CONNECTION TO THE DIVINE

The **12TH HOUSE** is the place of hidden things. This can speak to aspects of your life conducted in private, like the art you create for yourself. It can also describe the hidden parts of yourself, as in your unconscious mind. With your Rising sign ruler here, your life could be driven toward a life outside the public eye or to deep self-inquiry. In addition to personal hidden aspects, though, having your Rising sign ruler in the 12th House may steer your life toward engaging with things that are hidden from society more broadly—people who are incarcerated, marginalized populations, psychological research or practice, or perhaps engagement with the collective unconscious and dream interpretation.

This placement could also be interested in that which is hidden from sight in a physical sense, like being steered toward the study of microorganisms or subatomic particles. This house also pertains to spirituality and the hidden realms of the spirit, the Divine, and the afterlife.

129

DECODING YOUR RISING SIGN RULER'S HOUSE

➤ How is your life steered toward that which is hidden?

➤ How do solitude and self-reflection support a sense of purpose in your life?

➤ How does your life's motivation, described by your Rising sign (chapter 3), drive you to engage with the topics of the 12th House?

DECODING THE STARS

bell hooks

BIRTH DATE: September 25, 1952

BIRTH TIME: 8:57 p.m.

BIRTH LOCATION: Hopkinsville, Kentucky

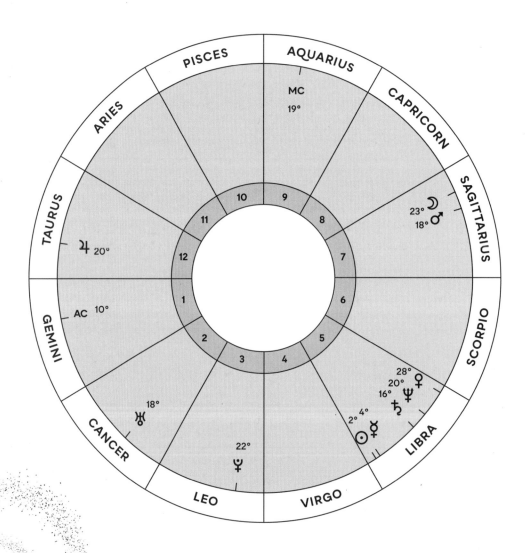

A feminist, activist, scholar, author, and professor, **bell hooks** was committed to an intellectual life that relentlessly and incisively interrogated social inequities precipitated by sexism, racism, and economic disparity. With Gemini as her Rising sign, we would expect her to live a life of the mind, one driven by insatiable curiosity and interest in a variety of topics.

With her Rising sign ruler in the 5th House (alongside her Sun and a number of planets), hooks's motivation to investigate and cogitate was directed toward her creative expression, evidenced through her writing and other creative endeavors. The influence of Gemini multiplicity is seen in the sheer quantity and range of her creative output: she authored more than thirty books—including scholarship, poetry, and children's books—and hundreds of articles; she presented at conferences; gave interviews on television and radio, including the *Ricki Lake Show*; and was featured in a number of documentaries.

A key goal in her varied creative outlets was to connect her message to her various audiences. In a 1994 interview with *BOMB Magazine*, hooks stressed the importance of using different approaches to writing to reach different audiences and effect change. Her focus on activism, equality, and social change through her creative works and by critiquing creative works is an expression of her Libra 5th House. A cultural studies scholar, hooks often trained her critical lens on film, music, television, and other artistic expressions in popular culture to unpack larger systemic issues. The centrality of this work to her life's purpose correlates to the placement of her Rising sign ruler in the 5th House.

DECODING THE STARS: bell hooks

CRACKING THE CODE
YOUR MOTIVATION

YOUR RISING SIGN

What motivates you? Which keywords or ideas from your Rising sign description resonate with you? Which don't?

What current activities in your personal or professional life align with this motivation and how do you feel when engaged in those activities?

What new activities do you feel called to and how does your desire to do them align with the motivation described by your Rising sign?

YOUR RISING SIGN + YOUR SUN SIGN

Do you resonate more with your Sun sign or your Rising sign?

In what ways do your Sun sign and your Rising sign work together? How does the motivation of your Rising sign support and enhance the way you shine?

In what ways do your Sun sign and Rising sign conflict or undermine each other? In what ways has this discord hampered you in the past? Can you think of ways to synthesize these attributes to bring you more joy and flow?

132

YOUR RISING SIGN RULER

Do you feel your life is steered by the energy and archetypal qualities of your Rising sign ruler?
Are you motivated by the same drives as your Rising sign ruler?

133

YOUR RISING SIGN RULER'S HOUSE + YOUR SUN HOUSE

How has your life been focused on the topics of your Sun's house? How has it been focused
on the topics of your Rising sign ruler's house? In what ways have the direction and themes of
your life synthesized the topics of both of these houses?

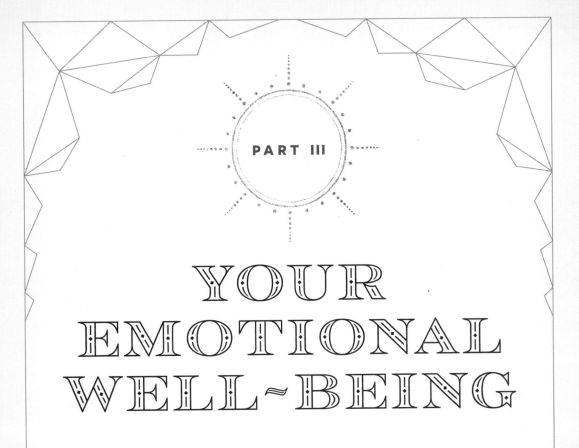

PART III

YOUR EMOTIONAL WELL~BEING

SO FAR IN OUR JOURNEY to decode your life's purpose we've considered your core nature (your Sun) and what motivates you to act (your Rising sign). Living a life of purpose, though, has a facet that is too often overlooked: emotional well-being. People land their dream jobs, fall in love, create families, go on adventures, and attempt to make all their dreams come true, and yet contentment evades them. Emotionally, they are whipped around, struggling to find equilibrium. You could attain all the trappings of your idealized life, but without emotional well-being, you'll find it hard to fully enjoy them.

What makes you feel emotionally safe and fulfilled? How can you bring yourself back to a place of emotional peace and stability when facing difficult emotions? There is a plethora of excellent resources on the psychology of emotional regulation that anyone would do well to dive into. But astrology, too, offers insight into your emotional nature and needs. By decoding your natal Moon placement, you can access guidance on how to cultivate your emotional well-being.

The sign of your natal Moon describes what makes you feel emotionally safe, secure, and satisfied. Your Moon house speaks to the areas in life in which you find emotional fulfillment. In this section, we'll delve into your Moon sign and house to better understand your emotional nature and how it is a critical element in decoding your life's purpose.

Your Moon Sign

YOUR EMOTIONAL NATURE

THE MOON IS the closest celestial body to Earth. It pulls on the oceans, the Earth's crust, and our own bodies with its gravitational force. Its influence on our physical world can be observed in phenomena like the daily ocean tides, but one of the Moon's most important effects on our planet is less immediately apparent. The Earth is tilted on an axis at about 23 degrees. The part of the Earth tilting toward the Sun is warmer than the part tilted away. Which hemisphere is angled toward or away from the Sun shifts as we make our annual trek around our star, resulting in our seasons. Our axial tilt is not fixed, however. Instead, the Earth shifts to and fro, changing the angle of tilt by a couple of degrees over tens of thousands of years. Even that small shift in the Earth's tilt has major implications for our global climate and is a key cause of Earth's ice ages. Without the influence of the Moon's gravity, the tilt of the Earth would fluctuate more significantly, leading to calamitous variations in Earth's climate. The Moon, then, plays a pivotal role in stabilizing our climate and the Earth's overall habitability.

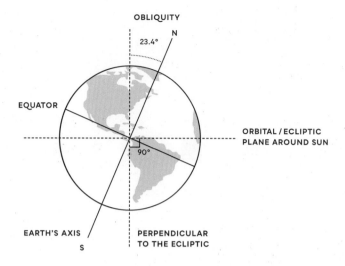

Likewise, in astrology, the Moon speaks to what regulates the shifting weather of your emotions and the means by which you can maintain emotional homeostasis. The zodiacal sign the Moon was in when you were born speaks to how you feel the most safe, secure, and fulfilled. This information can help you reflect on what you need to prioritize in your day-to-day life, relationships, and career to maintain emotional well-being. Interpreting your Moon sign can provide you with language to better understand your emotional nature and how to communicate your needs with others. This self-knowledge can ultimately help you maintain a more content and hopefully joyful life.

You may be tempted to gloss over this information. Often, emotions are seen as less important than matters of the mind or externally validated accomplishments. But in astrology, the Moon is a placement of high importance and is given essentially equal weight to your Sun sign. Though we know that the Moon is only a tiny fraction of the size of the Sun, from Earth's vantage point, they appear equal in size. They share dominion over the sky, over day and night. Indeed, the luminaries are inextricably linked, because the Moon shines by reflecting the Sun's light. Its borrowed light is no less important for its softness. In the dark of night and in the painful, hidden parts of ourselves, it is the Moon that lights our way home.

The Moon stabilizes the Earth and, similarly, the Moon in your chart explains how you can stabilize your own emotional well-being. However, it is important to note that stability doesn't mean a standstill. The Moon teaches us about the cyclical nature of inevitable change. The Moon waxes and wanes on a regular schedule. The Earth's axial tilt increases and decreases. Ice ages come and recede. Tides move in and out. Likewise, you become depleted and will again become full. You are brought low and again you'll soar high. The Moon teaches us to appreciate where we are in our cycle and know that it will pass. Sorrow and joy will wax and wane in their time. Your Moon sign will help you understand the phases of your emotions so you can understand what the ideal conditions are for you to feel emotionally full, versus the conditions that make you feel emotionally depleted. And just like the Moon's gravity holds the Earth in a balanced cycle that supports a sustainable, habitable climate, your Moon sign can help you understand how to keep your emotions from tilting too far askew.

137

YOUR LIFE'S PURPOSE AND YOUR MOON SIGN

What sort of work environment is best for you? When thinking about your life's purpose and your professional life, your Moon sign can help you understand what kinds of work environments will be challenging for you and which will feel supportive. This doesn't mean that you can't flourish in any work setting. Rather, if you know that your job will be challenging for you emotionally, understanding your Moon sign will help you identify what is taxing and help guide you toward ways of replenishing your emotional cup when it is empty. For each Moon sign, we'll consider **Strategies for Your Moon Sign** on how to use the gifts of the placement and ways to mitigate the more challenging aspects.

YOUR EMOTIONAL WELL-BEING

Fill in the blanks with information from your own birth chart.

Your Moon sign: _____

Your Moon sign element: _____

Your Moon sign modality: _____

MOON IN ARIES

ARIES MOON individuals have a fierce heart. Your emotions are big, brash, and powerful. There is a courageousness to how you love and how you care for those you love. How long your fuse is will depend on your Sun sign: if you are a fire or an air Sun sign, you'll more likely be quick-tempered, whereas if you are an earth or a water Sun sign (or a Libra), you may take a bit more effort to set off. But once your temper has been ignited, it's on. Anyone who knows an Aries Moon has seen it: jaw tight, shoulder set, glare fierce. You are a sight to behold when your warrior heart is called to action.

Once the fire is lit, it must burn until all the fuel is consumed. Aries Moon doesn't like to let their emotions simmer silently. Rather, you feel an almost undeniable urge to express your emotions. This can be wonderful when you're expressing joy or love, but can be problematic when your rage is inflamed. You find it necessary and satisfying to voice discontent when you've experienced a slight or injustice. Your anger flares brightly and just as quickly dissipates. More than other Moon placements, you can be quick to forgive once you've made your stand and exhausted the energy of your emotions. Generally, you are also less likely to hold grudges. It's important for people with Aries Moon to realize, though, that other Moon sign folks don't approach their emotions and conflict this way. While dealing with the issue immediately in the moment you feel emotionally activated may feel imperative to you, that may be anathema to the person you're arguing with. Others may shut down or walk away, leaving you frustrated because you haven't exhausted your emotional energy and there has been no resolution. Communicating to others that you prefer to deal with conflict immediately, and discussing how that might work with their approach to conflict, can help you clarify a way to productively address discord.

GET TO KNOW THEIR MOON SIGN

Knowing your Moon sign will help you understand how you emotionally regulate and relate to others. Understanding this will help you better communicate your emotional needs to friends and family so that they can interact with you in a way that supports your well-being and positive relationships. Likewise, getting to know the Moon signs of those you interact with will help you understand their emotional needs, how they work in harmony with your emotional disposition, and where you might differ. Especially when it comes to conflict, understanding someone's Moon sign will help you have more productive disagreements.

STRATEGIES FOR ARIES MOON

➤ **PICK YOUR BATTLES.** You have a gift of standing up for yourself and others, but sometimes this quality can be overactive, leading you to be overly sensitive and combative. Which arguments really matter? What outcome are you hoping to achieve by making a stand and will this argument aid in that goal?

➤ **FIND CONSTRUCTIVE WAYS TO GROUND INTENSE EMOTIONAL ENERGY.** Your emotions can burn hot, so finding ways to expel that energy will help clear your mind and enable you to act from a place of intention rather than reaction. What helps you release emotional energy? Is it vigorous physical activity or quiet solitude in nature? Do different emotions require different grounding methods? Keep a journal for a month and when you feel emotionally activated, see which activities bring you back to center. Which methods feel best?

➤ **CHANNEL YOUR WARRIOR ENERGY FOR GOOD.** You're not afraid of a fight and to call out injustice. How can you use this gift to help yourself and others?

MOON IN TAURUS

TAURUS MOON is most satisfied by simple pleasures: a gorgeous melody, a sumptuous sweater, a cozy blanket, a bouquet of flowers, a tasty picnic on a sunny day. When you are feeling overwhelmed, what are the pleasures that soothe you? Taurus is also a sign of building and craftsmanship. You may find that hobbies and crafts are essential to your well-being. Sewing, gardening, drawing, baking, or some other form of tactile craft will likely call to you and be a central strategy to emotionally regulate.

As important as the pleasure or craft itself is carving out enough time to enjoy it. Taurus Moon has its own pace and will not be rushed. It is likely that feeling rushed or pressured is what's causing you anxiety or frustration. A hallmark gift of Taurus is self-knowledge and the ability to set boundaries to protect their energy. However, if your Sun or Rising sign is more inclined toward people pleasing (e.g., Libra, Pisces) or a sense of duty to others (e.g., Cancer, Capricorn), you may need to work on learning your limits and how much time you need for self-care. Conversely, you may fall into the quintessential Taurus trap of excessive stubbornness. Perhaps being obstinate is emotionally satisfying to you, but it likely causes consternation in your relationships. Reflecting on your personal balance of give and take in relationships and how it influences your emotional well-being will be a useful practice.

Taurus is also the sign of substance and is the domain of financial systems. For you, monetary stability and material comforts are essential to your emotional well-being. Unfortunately, it's commonplace to have never learned even basic personal finance skills and many people are uncomfortable managing their money. This can lead to a great deal of daily stress and potentially debilitating financial strife. Working to heal your relationship with money and learning to manage your money will afford you indispensable peace and greatly improve your emotional well-being.

It must be noted that this is easier said than done. Generational poverty, privatized health care, overwhelming student loan debt, rampant inflation, and predatory mortgages are just a few of the factors contributing to widespread financial insecurity. Individual actions aren't enough to unseat the weight of systemic problems. Even so, addressing your relationship with money and cultivating healthy personal finance within your ability can aid your overall emotional well-being.

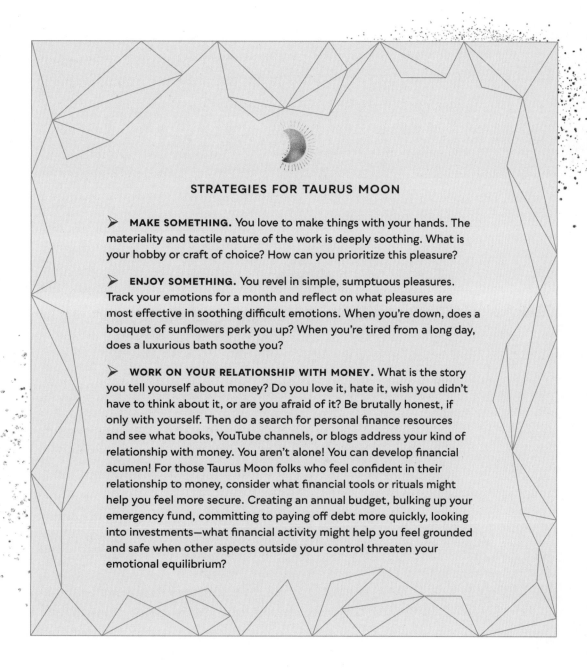

STRATEGIES FOR TAURUS MOON

➤ **MAKE SOMETHING.** You love to make things with your hands. The materiality and tactile nature of the work is deeply soothing. What is your hobby or craft of choice? How can you prioritize this pleasure?

➤ **ENJOY SOMETHING.** You revel in simple, sumptuous pleasures. Track your emotions for a month and reflect on what pleasures are most effective in soothing difficult emotions. When you're down, does a bouquet of sunflowers perk you up? When you're tired from a long day, does a luxurious bath soothe you?

➤ **WORK ON YOUR RELATIONSHIP WITH MONEY.** What is the story you tell yourself about money? Do you love it, hate it, wish you didn't have to think about it, or are you afraid of it? Be brutally honest, if only with yourself. Then do a search for personal finance resources and see what books, YouTube channels, or blogs address your kind of relationship with money. You aren't alone! You can develop financial acumen! For those Taurus Moon folks who feel confident in their relationship to money, consider what financial tools or rituals might help you feel more secure. Creating an annual budget, bulking up your emergency fund, committing to paying off debt more quickly, looking into investments—what financial activity might help you feel grounded and safe when other aspects outside your control threaten your emotional equilibrium?

143

MOON IN GEMINI

GEMINI MOON finds emotional satisfaction through following their curiosity down unexpected, winding paths and having engaging, quick, and far-ranging conversations. The world is vast and full of knowledge waiting to be uncovered and you feel a joyous, expansive lightness at the thought of it. Gemini is ruled by the planet Mercury, named for the Roman god of communication, travel, and commerce. Your Gemini Moon finds itself energized in places that feel like a bustling marketplace, where ideas and goods are traded at lightning speed. Mercury is also the god of tricksters and thieves, and Gemini Moon folks often have a mischievous streak. You have a willingness to play devil's advocate and take pleasure in asking provocative questions. It is the dance of the conversation that compels you more than even an answer, moving words like chess pieces, letting ideas skip across your tongue only to vanish, forgotten amid the deluge of all that follows.

Because it is your Moon that is placed here, there is an especially strong desire to communicate about emotions. You relate to emotions intellectually, unpacking them from every angle in your mind and with your friends, family, and romantic partners. Your upbringing may have instilled a sense of reserve around discussing emotions, but your innate desire still lies within you, dormant and waiting to be expressed. Give it a try with a person you trust and see how it feels. Does verbally expressing your emotions help bring you back to center, releasing anxiety that's been slowly collecting over years of repression? Perhaps the challenge is that you don't have the language to discuss all you feel. What books, videos, or resources can you immerse yourself in to broaden your knowledge?

A challenge of Gemini Moon can be talking in circles and never finding resolution. Mercury-ruled Moons (Gemini and Virgo) can both have a tendency toward anxious fixation. You may feel like you're getting somewhere in an argument just because you're talking it through, but you may

144

only be heightening your own worries and frustrating your friends. Digging into the research on effective communication could be a means of satisfying your curiosity, boosting your emotional self-knowledge, and improving your relationships.

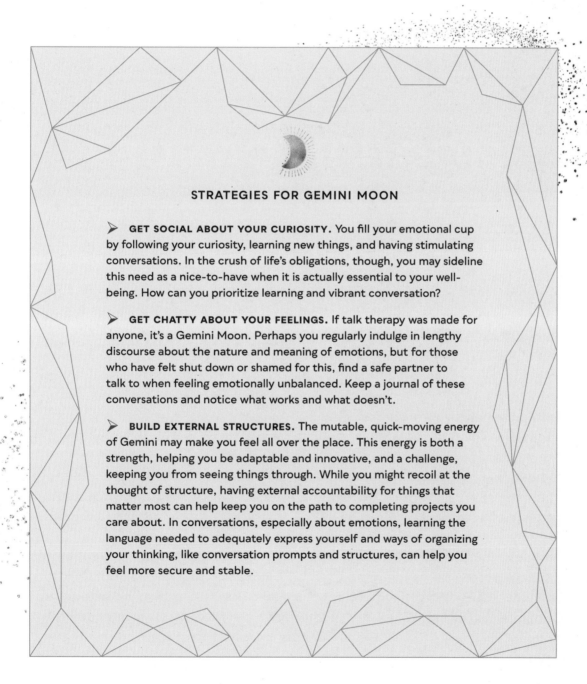

STRATEGIES FOR GEMINI MOON

➤ **GET SOCIAL ABOUT YOUR CURIOSITY.** You fill your emotional cup by following your curiosity, learning new things, and having stimulating conversations. In the crush of life's obligations, though, you may sideline this need as a nice-to-have when it is actually essential to your well-being. How can you prioritize learning and vibrant conversation?

➤ **GET CHATTY ABOUT YOUR FEELINGS.** If talk therapy was made for anyone, it's a Gemini Moon. Perhaps you regularly indulge in lengthy discourse about the nature and meaning of emotions, but for those who have felt shut down or shamed for this, find a safe partner to talk to when feeling emotionally unbalanced. Keep a journal of these conversations and notice what works and what doesn't.

➤ **BUILD EXTERNAL STRUCTURES.** The mutable, quick-moving energy of Gemini may make you feel all over the place. This energy is both a strength, helping you be adaptable and innovative, and a challenge, keeping you from seeing things through. While you might recoil at the thought of structure, having external accountability for things that matter most can help keep you on the path to completing projects you care about. In conversations, especially about emotions, learning the language needed to adequately express yourself and ways of organizing your thinking, like conversation prompts and structures, can help you feel more secure and stable.

145

MOON IN CANCER

CANCER MOON finds security and stability in meaningful relationships and in cultivating a sense of home. Cancer is the sign of family, ancestry, and home, and these domains are where your heart lies. You are devoted to your loved ones and can find it emotionally fulfilling to express your love through acts of service, holding space, and even thoughtful, nostalgic gifts. Your house might be the hub for your chosen community, in part because you love being at home and in part because your place feels like home to others. It also may be that you, personally, feel like home to others.

You may experience emotional volatility because you feel so much, but with your Moon residing in its home sign of Cancer, you also have the resources necessary to cultivate emotional well-being. The mistake is to think that emotional regulation means invariable consistency. The goal is not to achieve some sort of emotional flatlining. The Moon waxes and wanes. The seasons change. Plants grow, die, decay, and new growth begins again. The natural state of our world is cyclical and so, too, are your emotions. There will be a season for grief, and a season for joy—they might occur in the same day. The gift you share with the rest of the zodiac is illustrating the full and terrible beauty of the human emotional experience. While material accomplishments have their place, Cancer Moon knows that the content and quality of our lives are determined by what we feel. Love, connection, joy, pride, enthusiasm, sorrow, worry, regret—this is what our lives are made of.

Despite your rich emotional life, it's likely that only those closest to you will know what all goes on inside, because you keep your emotional turmoil locked up in your crabby shell. Perhaps your emotional volatility befuddles even you, especially if repression is your primary coping mechanism. Learning the language of emotions and taking the time to get to know the tides of your emotional ocean will be essential for you to cultivate well-being and to feel like you're living in flow with your emotions, rather than being pulled around by them.

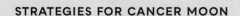

STRATEGIES FOR CANCER MOON

➤ **COMMUNICATE YOUR EXPECTATIONS.** Your Cancer Moon desires emotional connection and to show love through loyalty, duty, and creating a sense of home. It can be frustrating when those you love don't seem to appreciate how you show love or reciprocate in kind. People with air Moon signs may seem to not take things as seriously as you do. Earth Moon signs might be too cold and pragmatic. Learning to communicate your emotional needs and expectations can help you have more satisfying relationships and ultimately improve your overall well-being.

➤ **TRACK YOUR EMOTIONS.** Your hard shell that protects your soft center may keep others from seeing your true feelings, but it may also prevent you from understanding what you're feeling and why. Keeping a journal of your emotions and the circumstances surrounding those emotions can help improve your self-knowledge and find ways to mitigate emotional volatility.

➤ **HONOR YOUR EMOTIONS.** You may have internalized messages from family or society that expressing emotions is a weakness. Trying to excessively control emotions leads to an antagonistic relationship with your feelings that can be frustrating, causing an internal monologue of self-chastisement for not "having it together." Approaching your emotions with compassion and embracing the full spectrum of human experience can help alleviate some of the pressure to control.

147

MOON IN LEO

LEO MOON feels emotionally satisfied and rejuvenated when given ample attention and adoration. Leo is associated with the archetype of the performer, and you derive pleasure from entertaining and basking in your well-earned applause. The desired size of your audience will be influenced by your Moon house placement (e.g., if your Moon is in the 4th House, your preferred audience is likely your family, whereas 10th or 11th House Leo Moons will be interested in a much larger, public audience).

The placement of your natal Sun, which is the ruling luminary of Leo, will also give you information as to the style and places you like to shine. Because of the Sun-Leo connection, there is an inextricable link between shining your authentic light in the world and your emotional well-being.

Even though your Leonine heart relishes acknowledgment for shining your bright, beautiful self, you're not only self-interested. Like the Sun, your warm nature is life-giving to those around you. You fill your emotional cup through generosity, likely giving your emotional support and love. Perhaps gift giving is a major love language for you. A pitfall some Leo Moons fall into is using generosity to curry favor and connection, which will ultimately lead to shallow relationships and hollow praise. Owning your true nature and finding those who enthusiastically love you for who you are is the pathway to satisfying relationships.

STRATEGIES FOR LEO MOON

➤ **STUDY YOUR SUN SIGN AND HOUSE.** Your Leo Moon compels you to desire recognition for your authentic expression of self. Understanding your whole chart (and reading this book!) will help you reflect on who you are here to be and what you are here to do. Because Leo is ruled by the Sun, though, your emotional well-being is more deeply tied to your Sun placement than that for any other Moon placement. Understanding the style in which you want to shine in the world (Sun sign) and the places in life you most feel called to shine (your Sun house) will help you understand the kinds of activities that will fill your emotional cup.

➤ **OWN YOUR STAGE.** Leo placements get a lot of flak for owning their awesomeness. Perhaps you've never fully identified with your Leo Moon placement because society has impressed upon you that it is a great sin of unconscionable ego to take up space and fully be who you are. It's time to expel that rhetoric from your programming and claim your true nature. Be who you are on the stages that call to you, whether that's in the classroom, boardroom, Senate floor, or center stage. It's easier said than done, so if you struggle to shine authentically for yourself, then do it so that others can stop extinguishing their flame to conform to society's narrow standards.

➤ **BE GENEROUS.** One of the easiest ways to fill your emotional cup is to be generous with others. You have a warm, giving nature and likely you know what kinds of generosity you most enjoy and what others most appreciate from you. Is it your time, your humor, your words of encouragement, your sympathetic ear, your warm hugs? When feeling emotionally drained, you may feel the need to withdraw, but perhaps try counteracting sadness or malaise with kindness. You may find that the act of giving is a gift to yourself as well.

MOON IN VIRGO

VIRGO MOON individuals fill their emotional cup by organizing, perfecting, and being of service. Virgo is an earth sign ruled by Mercury and brings the mental swiftness and acuity signified by that planet into the material realm by amending inefficiencies and errors. You find it soothing to give in to the Virgoan drive to fix things and get your ducks in a row. There is a busy, buzzing energy to Virgo that has you flitting from one project to the next. Nothing is so emotionally satisfying to you as crossing another task off your to-do list. This can-do attitude is amplified when you are emotionally activated. No one would be surprised to find you deep-cleaning your oven or organizing your closet when stressed.

You likely don't find it easy to relax. There is always something that needs doing. Whenever you try to enjoy doing nothing, your mind can plague you with worried ruminations about what you have yet to do or what you could have done better. You may pick over each minute detail of conversations you've had or work you've submitted and think of how you could have done it better. Your mind may be prone to getting in loops about how future events might go or tasks you must complete. Mindfulness practices and breathing exercises could help you learn to quiet your mind and be in the moment, but your mind may be too busy for these to bring relief. Exercise and physical projects like cleaning can help get you out of your head and into your body when your stress levels are high.

Virgo Moons express love through acts of service. Caring for others, especially for their physical health and well-being, is a trait of Virgo. Virgo Moons, therefore, show affection by taking care of others and trying to help fix their problems. This makes you a reliable and helpful friend who no doubt is much appreciated by those lucky enough to have been helped by you. Things can go awry, though, when your perfectionist eye is turned toward your loved ones. You want the best for those you care about, and you do actually know what you're talking about, but not everyone is capable or willing to endure your sharp scrutiny and exacting standards. When you are feeling stressed and in need of something to fix, it's best to avoid nitpicking the people in your life. Remember that your friends, family, and romantic partners are people, not projects.

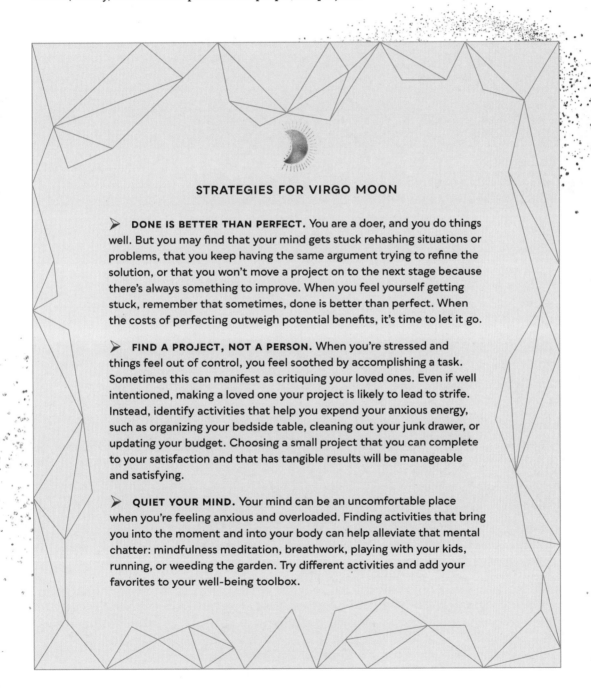

STRATEGIES FOR VIRGO MOON

➤ **DONE IS BETTER THAN PERFECT.** You are a doer, and you do things well. But you may find that your mind gets stuck rehashing situations or problems, that you keep having the same argument trying to refine the solution, or that you won't move a project on to the next stage because there's always something to improve. When you feel yourself getting stuck, remember that sometimes, done is better than perfect. When the costs of perfecting outweigh potential benefits, it's time to let it go.

➤ **FIND A PROJECT, NOT A PERSON.** When you're stressed and things feel out of control, you feel soothed by accomplishing a task. Sometimes this can manifest as critiquing your loved ones. Even if well intentioned, making a loved one your project is likely to lead to strife. Instead, identify activities that help you expend your anxious energy, such as organizing your bedside table, cleaning out your junk drawer, or updating your budget. Choosing a small project that you can complete to your satisfaction and that has tangible results will be manageable and satisfying.

➤ **QUIET YOUR MIND.** Your mind can be an uncomfortable place when you're feeling anxious and overloaded. Finding activities that bring you into the moment and into your body can help alleviate that mental chatter: mindfulness meditation, breathwork, playing with your kids, running, or weeding the garden. Try different activities and add your favorites to your well-being toolbox.

151

MOON IN LIBRA

152

LIBRA MOON individuals are soothed by peace and beauty. Unless you have significant placements that have a comfort with conflict (e.g., your Sun or Rising sign in Aries, Taurus, Capricorn, or Gemini), you are likely thrown off-kilter by discord and avoid it at all costs. To a lesser degree, incivility and impropriety are off-putting and you strive to avoid crass people and situations. You are emotionally soothed by harmony and beauty. Identifying a few go-to soothing activities will help you maintain emotional equilibrium in a noisy, chaotic world: making your home a lovely retreat, taking a luxuriant bath, or enjoying your favorite music can soothe your Venusian nature. Most especially, though, taking a break from other humans is an important strategy. Libra Moon can tend to people please and is sensitive to conflict. Sometimes the only way to reset and replenish from interpersonal burnout is solitude.

Because of your desire and ability to broker balance and peace, you could end up the resident mediator of your friends and family. You may find this emotionally satisfying, with the reward of resolution outweighing the discomfort of discord. This may extend to your professional life, even, in a position that uses your skills of diplomacy, litigation, or mediation. The risk, though, is that you may find yourself uncomfortably in the middle of other people's problems and not know how to extricate yourself. Learning what your limits are and how to say no are essential skills for you.

One thing to remember is that the scales of Libra are always striving for balance, but that isn't a static state you can maintain. Balance is a process, not a location. Be kind to yourself when you feel emotionally out of whack. Get comfortable with recalibrating and accept that you often will go too far one way before you realize you need to pull back or switch gears.

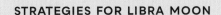

STRATEGIES FOR LIBRA MOON

➤ **CREATE A RESTORATIVE TOOLBOX.** What activities help you experience Venusian respite from crude reality? What beauty, harmony, and peace can you cultivate? Libra Moon can have expensive tastes, but remember that peace and beauty can be inexpensive or free.

➤ **LEARN YOUR LIMITS.** People pleasing can be a challenge for you. On the one hand, you dislike conflict, and on the other, you greatly enjoy making people happy and creating harmonious relationships and environments. But always trying to anticipate other people's needs or trying to avoid disagreements at all costs will eventually exhaust you. Get familiar with what it feels like when you start getting depleted so that you can course correct and say no when you have no more you're willing to give. When it comes to boundaries, there are some hard lines you can draw, but more nuanced is figuring out how to communicate when you're just unavailable or tapped out for now. It's okay to not do something this time that you have done before. Balancing is a process.

➤ **PUT YOUR VENUSIAN GIFTS TO USE.** You're a gifted diplomat and have tasteful aesthetic judgment. Finding outlets for your Venusian skills beyond your home and self-care can be a path to emotional fulfillment. In what parts of your life do you already employ your diplomacy and taste? What would you like to do more of?

153

MOON IN SCORPIO

SCORPIO MOON folks are a bit of a paradox. You are a very private person, keeping your emotions close to the vest and allowing only a select few to get under your exoskeleton. For those you do let in, you desire and demand deep emotional intimacy. While you aren't necessarily forthcoming with others about how you're feeling or what's on your mind, you're interested in and adept at drawing out the secrets of others. This stems in part from your desire for emotional intimacy, but also from your emotional need for the truth. You feel compelled to know what others are trying to hide and what lies beneath. Traditionally ruled by Mars, your hard shell serves as your shield to keep people at arm's length while your stinger functions like a spear, cutting to the heart of the truth. Mostly likely you've honed your mind and tongue to pierce through others' emotional armor, while also being able to deflect their attempts to get under your skin.

For some Scorpio Moons, this is about power plays and subterfuge. You have an innate understanding of power dynamics and may relish the machinations of corporate maneuvering or interpersonal drama. For most Scorpio Moons, though, it's less dramatic than that. You are private because your business is your own. People have to earn your trust to gain access to your inner world, and you don't give that up lightly. As opposed to Scorpio Sun sign individuals whose search for truth is core to their nature and may manifest in many areas of their life (personal or professional), your Scorpio Moon is most interested in honesty and loyalty from your loved ones. Scorpio Moon is known to hold a grudge and to go for the jugular when provoked, which is your prerogative. But Scorpio Moon also displays impressive devotion to those they deem worthy.

Scorpio's modern ruler is Pluto, named for the god of the Underworld. Pluto's significations include power, oppression, that which is buried or hidden, death, transformation, and rebirth. How these topics prove meaningful to each Scorpio Moon will vary. Look to the house in which your Moon is placed to see which areas of life the topics of power and transformation will be most potent. Some Scorpio Moons live out these Plutonic themes in creating or being drawn to art that deals with them. Others may serve as a guide for people on their underworld journeys as therapists or coaches, who help their clients uncover what is hidden in their unconscious mind. Similarly, editors, agents, and directors serve as companions to creatives through the transformative process of birthing their work. Having your Moon in Scorpio means you are gifted with the ability to cut to the truth, the fortitude to sit with difficult emotional material, and the magic to facilitate transformation (for yourself or others).

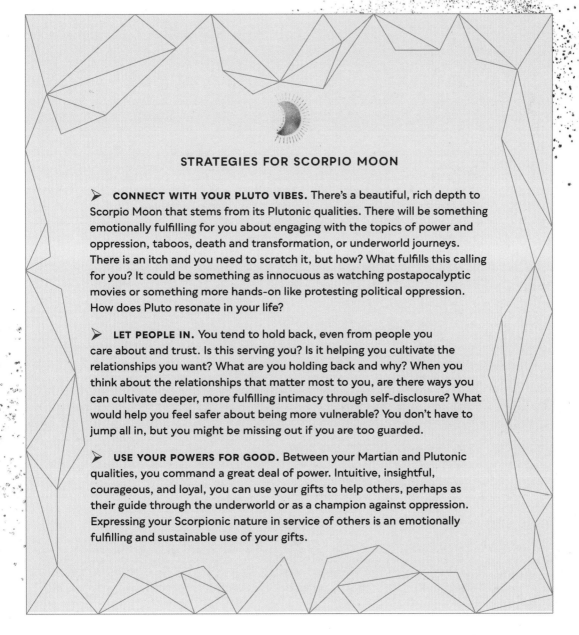

STRATEGIES FOR SCORPIO MOON

➤ **CONNECT WITH YOUR PLUTO VIBES.** There's a beautiful, rich depth to Scorpio Moon that stems from its Plutonic qualities. There will be something emotionally fulfilling for you about engaging with the topics of power and oppression, taboos, death and transformation, or underworld journeys. There is an itch and you need to scratch it, but how? What fulfills this calling for you? It could be something as innocuous as watching postapocalyptic movies or something more hands-on like protesting political oppression. How does Pluto resonate in your life?

➤ **LET PEOPLE IN.** You tend to hold back, even from people you care about and trust. Is this serving you? Is it helping you cultivate the relationships you want? What are you holding back and why? When you think about the relationships that matter most to you, are there ways you can cultivate deeper, more fulfilling intimacy through self-disclosure? What would help you feel safer about being more vulnerable? You don't have to jump all in, but you might be missing out if you are too guarded.

➤ **USE YOUR POWERS FOR GOOD.** Between your Martian and Plutonic qualities, you command a great deal of power. Intuitive, insightful, courageous, and loyal, you can use your gifts to help others, perhaps as their guide through the underworld or as a champion against oppression. Expressing your Scorpionic nature in service of others is an emotionally fulfilling and sustainable use of your gifts.

MOON IN SAGITTARIUS

SAGITTARIUS MOON is an optimistic, adventurous heart. Your emotional buoyancy is nigh indefatigable and a gift to you and those around you. This isn't to say that you don't ever feel sad or depressed. Jupiter is the ruler of Sagittarius and imbues the sign with luck and optimism, yes, but also expansion. There is a feeling of *more* with Jupiter, and that may translate to big feelings, both highs and lows. But your natural emotional state is one of hope and playfulness.

What gets you down is monotony and restriction. You don't want to be held down, doing the same thing day in and day out. Your well-being requires adventure, whatever that means for you. It is true that many Sagittarians enjoy long-distance travel, new locales, and even adrenaline-pumping excitement, but adventure could be closer to home in local hiking trails or even through books and courses of study. While the novelty of adventure brings you special joy, you'll need a steadier, more reliable form of adventure to replenish your emotional well. You likely already know what your preferred type of adventure is, though keep in mind that this can evolve throughout your life. Rifling through the stacks of used bookstores, surfing, going for a drive, or walking in your local parks are just a few activities that could make your heart sing. Making time for these activities each week will go a long way to support your well-being.

What Sagittarius is seeking in all their adventures is a transcendent experience, some higher truth, a glimpse of the Divine. Sometimes this transcendence is experienced through high-risk adventure or strenuous physical activity. You may find it by experiencing diverse places and people, seeing the divine connection in the similarities and differences among cultures. For others, this seeking may be more cerebral, leading you down a path of intellectual inquiry, whether formally in school or informally following your own curiosity. This drive often involves some form of spirituality, however you define it. Because of this, some form of spiritual practice can be particularly soothing and fulfilling for Sagittarius Moon.

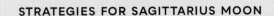

STRATEGIES FOR SAGITTARIUS MOON

➤ **FIND AN ADVENTURE.** Even with variability at work, your thirst for adventure will likely not be satiated in your professional life. The Sagittarian drive for adventure doesn't necessitate a passport and spending lots of money on expensive trips, however. Finding adventures in your everyday life will help you feel emotionally fulfilled. What calls to you? Is it visiting different local restaurants, museums, or outdoor spaces? Is it meeting new people through community groups? Is it scratching the adrenaline itch through extreme sports on the weekends? How can you prioritize adventure in your life every week?

➤ **SEEK OUT OPTIMISM.** Your warm, hopeful heart is a bright light to the world, but even you can feel diminished by the bitterness and strife of reality. What activities reinvigorate your sense of optimism? Perhaps it is a bouquet of sunflowers, or a spiritual practice, or a gratitude list. What small activities renew your spark of hope?

➤ **GET SPIRITUAL.** Your emotional well-being is influenced by the Sagittarian drive to find spiritual truth and experience transcendence. Cultivating a spiritual practice will be particularly important, in whatever way is meaningful to you. This doesn't mean following a specific religious tradition, necessarily. Being in nature, listening to or creating music, engaging with philosophy, meditating, running, praying—any activity that feels spiritual and nourishing to you is what matters.

157

MOON IN CAPRICORN

CAPRICORN MOON is the heart of the achiever. Setting goals and accomplishing them is supremely satisfying. While this is true for many, it is imperative for you. Capricorn is ruled by Saturn, the planet of systems, boundaries, structures, and order, so what helps replenish your emotional well is completing benchmarks along a defined path toward a specific goal. Lack of structure and vague targets are annoying and unsettling to you. You want to know where you stand, how far you've come, and how far you have yet to go.

Saturn is also the planet of tradition. Most Capricorn Moons find comfort in traditional, externally validated forms of accomplishment. A major exception is those born between 1989 and 1996 (and a few months in 1988), who have Uranus in Capricorn. For these individuals, there can be a strong desire to break with tradition, because Uranus is the planet of revolution and rebellion. If you are one of these individuals with Uranus and your Moon in Capricorn, you may face an internal struggle between the desire for individuality and a yearning for more conventional ideals of stability.

While working toward a goal is paramount to Capricorn Moons, the Saturnian desire for structure more generally is also important to you. When you feel emotionally unmoored, you can ground yourself in daily structures and habits, such as a set morning routine—whatever structures help you feel contained and safe. Limiting uncertainty through routine is soothing to you, but so too is limiting choice. Saturn is the planet of restriction, and a positive way of working with this aspect of your Moon sign is to simplify and focus. Decision fatigue and general overwhelm can be assuaged by cutting out or putting on pause certain activities to allow your limited energy to be focused on what matters most.

STRATEGIES FOR CAPRICORN MOON

➤ **MAKE A PATHWAY TO SUCCESS.** You need goals to feel fulfilled. What are your goals and what are the interim achievements to get there? You can create road maps to success in any aspect of life: work, hobbies, travel, or learning. Whenever you feel emotionally frazzled, come back to one of your road maps and review what you've accomplished and what your next step is. See if you can take a step toward getting to your next achievement. Reminding yourself of what you have accomplished and taking steps toward new achievements will help you feel emotionally centered.

➤ **CUT THINGS OUT.** When you are feeling overwhelmed, figure out what you can take off your plate. This may seem counterintuitive, because you love to accomplish tasks, but you can easily have too many goals you're working toward. When things get hectic, see which activities you need to prioritize and which activities can be paused. It's okay to say no. It's okay to table things until later.

➤ **FIND AN ENDURANCE ACTIVITY.** Capricorn is about effort toward a goal, and as an earth sign, the priority is endurance over speed. Physical activity can provide a useful means of emotional regulation, and for you, something that requires time and effort toward staying power and defined achievements will be especially fulfilling. Long walks, marathons, powerlifting, meditation, yoga, swimming laps, rock climbing—any activity that you approach with methodical determination to improve endurance and strength will be especially fulfilling.

MOON IN AQUARIUS

AQUARIUS MOON folks approach emotions—their own and the feelings of others—from an intellectual, 30,000-foot level. Aquarius is an air sign whose traditional ruler is disciplined Saturn. As such, Aquarius seeks to filter emotions through the analytical sieve of the mind, putting each facial expression, joyful outburst, and argument into its corresponding box. Whereas water and fire signs are more apt to focus on the experience of emotional responses, Aquarius wants to philosophize, wants to understand what makes that emotion tick, wants to fit it into a schema. Trying to impose a rigid structure on human emotions, however, is a fool's errand. Yes, developing a language to describe emotions is valuable, and identifying the causes and cures of difficult emotions is worthwhile and will help you feel more secure emotionally. But believing that X action leads to Y emotion to be ameliorated by Z behavior should always be true is going to leave you frustrated. Aquarius Moon is looking for the logic of emotions, but emotions aren't that logical. This intellectualizing can be off-putting to others. They may want you to just accept that's how they feel, but you want to have a concrete reason why they feel that way, leading to discord and frustration.

Alternatively, the intellectual detachment of your Moon sign may mean that you feel disconnected from your own emotions. You may struggle to know or verbalize how you feel. The modern ruler of Aquarius is Uranus, and there is an outsider quality to this energy. You may feel alienated from your own emotions and struggle to relate when others are expressing how they are feeling. Learning about ways to access and ground your emotions in your body through mindfulness meditation or somatic therapy could be useful in helping you connect with your emotions.

The gifts of this placement are that your emotional distance enables you to keep a level head in challenging situations. When emotions run high, you are less encumbered and can stay focused on finding resolution. You feel emotionally fulfilled when situations are parsed into a logical

160

understanding from which a plan of action can be built. Aquarius is the sign of collective humanity and progress, so you also may have a drive to help society move forward and the emotional fortitude to make a difference.

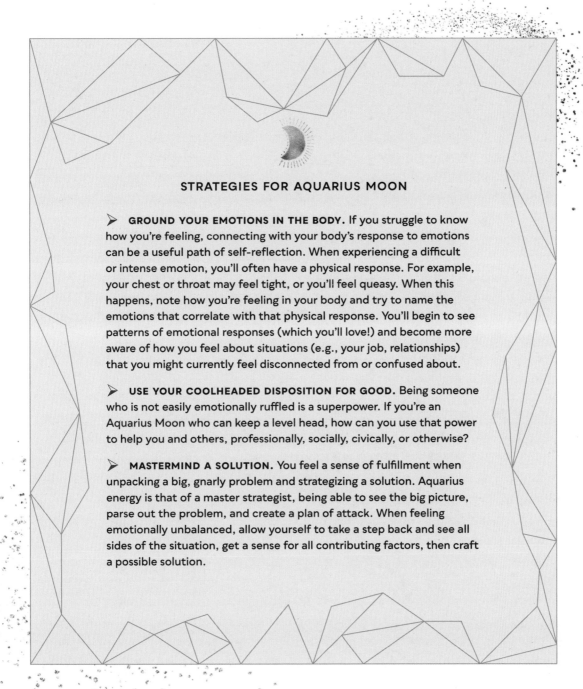

STRATEGIES FOR AQUARIUS MOON

➤ **GROUND YOUR EMOTIONS IN THE BODY.** If you struggle to know how you're feeling, connecting with your body's response to emotions can be a useful path of self-reflection. When experiencing a difficult or intense emotion, you'll often have a physical response. For example, your chest or throat may feel tight, or you'll feel queasy. When this happens, note how you're feeling in your body and try to name the emotions that correlate with that physical response. You'll begin to see patterns of emotional responses (which you'll love!) and become more aware of how you feel about situations (e.g., your job, relationships) that you might currently feel disconnected from or confused about.

➤ **USE YOUR COOLHEADED DISPOSITION FOR GOOD.** Being someone who is not easily emotionally ruffled is a superpower. If you're an Aquarius Moon who can keep a level head, how can you use that power to help you and others, professionally, socially, civically, or otherwise?

➤ **MASTERMIND A SOLUTION.** You feel a sense of fulfillment when unpacking a big, gnarly problem and strategizing a solution. Aquarius energy is that of a master strategist, being able to see the big picture, parse out the problem, and create a plan of attack. When feeling emotionally unbalanced, allow yourself to take a step back and see all sides of the situation, get a sense for all contributing factors, then craft a possible solution.

MOON IN PISCES

PISCES MOON is the heart of the lover, artist, and mystic. The nature of Pisces is to dissolve boundaries and feel connected, to experience the truth that we are all one: one people, one ecosystem, one planet, one collection of atoms in a universe of atoms, one spirit connected to a Universal Spirit. This knowledge of connection imbues you with a deep capacity for love and compassion. Where some people stand in judgment of others, you see individuals as inherently worthy and from this position you are uniquely able to witness and love others.

There is a drive in your heart for this sense of ego dissolution and connection. This can be achieved through many methods, including meditation, spiritual practice, and creating or experiencing art and music. One archetype that Pisces is correlated with is the artist because art allows us to step outside ourselves, experience the world from a different viewpoint, and recognize the fragile artifice of our constructed reality in the microcosm of the painting, the stage, or the poem. And like the mystic, whose practices enable them to connect with divine wisdom and transcendent experience, the artist, too, has some portal to divine inspiration that they access when they create.

But there is a negative expression of this drive for dissolution, where escapism is sought through substance abuse or unhealthy romantic attachment. The allure of losing yourself in addiction or dissolving into another person can be heady, but ultimately dangerous. There are such beautiful, fulfilling ways to tap into the feeling of connection you seek—visual art, music, movies, books, and spiritual experiences being chief among them. The simplest form of escapism that you can enjoy is allowing your imagination to wander. Daydreaming is a potent form of self-care for a Pisces Moon.

Your Pisces Moon heart is depleted most by simply having to be human and facing the brutal onslaught of reality. It is exhausting. Though other Moon signs may also feel worn thin by life, they can't quite understand the way it is exhausting for you. Perhaps they want a vacation. You want to astral project out of your body. Finding safe, soothing, perhaps creative ways to step out of yourself will enable you to replenish your emotional well.

STRATEGIES FOR PISCES MOON

➤ **HARNESS THE POWER OF IMAGINATION.** You possess a powerful imagination and a direct line to inspiration. While imagination is a valuable approach to maintaining your well-being, it can also be useful in the workplace. How can your creativity and collective viewpoint be part of your work?

➤ **SEEK SOLITUDE.** Although you love meaningful connection with others, you are likely to get emotionally depleted and require regular blocks of solitude and rest. It is okay to say no. Staying home to do nothing is a valid choice.

➤ **COMMIT TO A SPIRITUAL PRACTICE.** What helps you tap into that sublime feeling of the enormity of the universe and the smallness of self? What helps you dull the noise of the mundane and stand in awe of something infinite? Physics, music, spiritual practice—whatever calls to you, relish and replenish in it.

163

Your Moon House

WHERE YOU FIND
EMOTIONAL FULFILLMENT

IN THE PREVIOUS CHAPTER, we covered how your Moon sign describes your emotional needs and gives insight into what stresses you out and how you can get back to emotional equilibrium. In this chapter, we'll look at the house your Moon is in, which describes where in life you find emotional fulfillment.

Recall that the birth chart is broken up into twelve houses and each of those houses corresponds to different topics of life. Your Moon can fall in any house and the topics of your Moon house describe the places in your life that are most emotionally satisfying and nourishing to you. It's where you come back to recharge if you feel emotionally tapped out.

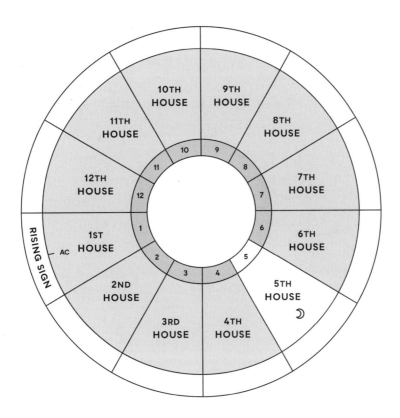

What do I mean by emotional fulfillment? We all know what it is to feel burned out. We get stretched too thin, have too much work to do, have had too many social interactions, or go through emotionally strenuous life events. We get depleted. Your Moon sign (chapter 5) tells you what is likely to deplete you and gives insight into how to soothe yourself and find emotional stability. Your Moon house tells you where in life you find emotional support and joy. When you feel depleted and need to replenish your emotional well, it'll be by engaging in the activities described by your Moon house.

Let's consider an example. Say someone has their Moon in their 5th House. The 5th House is the place of creativity and children in the birth chart. Someone with their Moon here would find emotional fulfillment by engaging in creative projects—hobbies, art, or however they feel most creative. This individual may also feel emotionally fulfilled by their relationships with their children, or perhaps in working with children (as a teacher, for example). The way that the person is creative or how they like to connect with their children will be described by their Moon sign.

Understanding your Moon sign and house and your emotional nature is critical to living a purposeful life since feeling satisfaction is, after all, an emotional state. No amount of meaningful work or accomplishments will create a fulfilling life if you are constantly depleted, exhausted, or depressed. Becoming the expert on your own emotional well-being is a lifelong journey, but hopefully understanding your natal Moon will give you a starting point and some language to think about your emotional needs.

You can tackle this chapter by first checking out the Moon House Quick Guide for an overview of the meaning of your Moon house. Then, read your specific Moon house description in this chapter for more detail. Afterwards, check out the section entitled **Cracking the Code: Your Emotional Well-being** to reflect on how you can apply this astrological wisdom in your life.

YOUR MOON HOUSE QUICK GUIDE

MOON HOUSE	You find emotional fulfillment and live out your purpose day-to-day through . . .
1	focusing on personal growth, self-expression, and caring for your body.
2	your work and cultivating financial independence.
3	communication, such as writing, speaking, teaching, and/or artistic expression.
4	cultivating your home space, spending time with your family, and/or helping others build home and family.
5	your creative pursuits, raising your children, and/or working with children.
6	cultivating nourishing, productive daily routines and habits.
7	meaningful, committed partnership (romantic, platonic, and business).
8	transformational experiences and tending to your mental health.
9	traveling, learning, and teaching.
10	building your career and legacy.
11	spending time with friends, building community, and/or cultivating clients and patrons.
12	personal introspection and/or spiritual experiences.

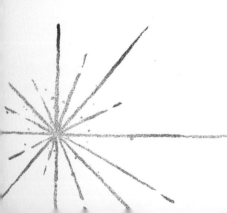

DECODING HOUSE PLACEMENTS

Your Moon House is a key component to understanding your life's purpose. It explains where you find emotional fulfillment and gives information about how you live out your life's purpose on a day-to-day basis. But your Moon's house placement is only one part of the story. Understanding the house your Rising sign ruler is placed in (chapter 4) and the house your Sun occupies (chapter 2) are also important considerations for what areas of life are most critical for you. After reading about those three placements, you can blend and balance the meaning of those houses. See the final section, **Calibration**, for an example.

YOUR EMOTIONAL WELL-BEING

Fill in the blank with information from your own birth chart.

Your Moon house: _____

MOON IN THE 1st HOUSE

EMOTIONAL FULFILLMENT THROUGH FOCUSING ON PERSONAL GROWTH, SELF-EXPRESSION, AND CARING FOR YOUR BODY

The **1st HOUSE** is the place of self—your identity, your body, your self-image. To have your Moon here means that your emotional well-being is intimately tied to your sense of self. This can be a challenging placement, as your identity will always be under some pressure from external forces to conform to various societal standards. Having your Moon here could speak to being especially sensitive to how you are perceived by others and how you cultivate your image. What is helpful to remember is that we are always in flux and always growing. You have the ability to shape yourself into an identity that feels most true and nourishing to you. Attending to your self-care and personal development will be fulfilling and help you maintain emotional equilibrium. The more you consciously reflect on who you are and intentionally cultivate who you want to be, the more secure and satisfied you'll feel.

168

It may be helpful to consider the element of your 1st House sign in order to understand your approach to self and how your identity influences your emotional needs. If your 1st House element is earth, you'll likely identify as being pragmatic and grounded. You'll feel emotional security when you can construct a clear sense of self with identifiable boundaries. If your 1st House element is air, you may take a fluid, philosophical approach to self. Emotionally, you'll appreciate freedom to shift your self-concept and would benefit from intellectual self-reflection (journaling, for example). Water signs in the 1st House seek emotional depth and interpersonal connection. Your water Moon will appreciate a self-concept that isn't overly stoic, but rather embraces the full range of emotions. Your Moon in a fire sign in the 1st House would be interested in a self-concept of individuality, freedom, and autonomy. Look to your specific Moon sign to learn more about the nature of your emotional needs.

DECODING YOUR MOON'S HOUSE

➢ What ideas about who you are and who you should be have you internalized from family, friends, and society? Which of these ideas feels true to who you are? Which ideas need to be released?

➢ What regular practices of self-reflection do you engage in (e.g., journaling, therapy, spiritual practice)?

➢ How can you approach self-reflection and development from a loving, nonjudgmental space?

EMOTIONAL FULFILLMENT THROUGH YOUR WORK AND CULTIVATING FINANCIAL INDEPENDENCE

The **2ND HOUSE** is the place of your money and assets. It speaks to how you support yourself and acquire the material sustenance of life. With your Moon here, your emotional well-being and security are intimately tied to your financial, material security. Ensuring that you can provide for yourself will be essential in your life. When feeling stressed or emotionally volatile, you'll find equilibrium through attending to your personal finances. You may find that regularly reviewing your budgeting spreadsheet is your favorite self-care activity.

You may have a complicated relationship with money. Most people do. Rarely do people learn healthy financial habits early in life and we are bombarded with conflicting narratives about how much money we should make, how we should manage it, and what we should spend it on.

The challenges of our modern society—rife with debt, inflation, job insecurity, skyrocketing housing costs, and unaffordable healthcare—make it impossible for most of us to feel monetarily secure. For you, developing a workable, positive relationship with how you sustain yourself is imperative. This doesn't mean embracing capitalist narratives or striving to be the next Rockefeller. Having the Moon in the 2nd House isn't about accruing wealth. Rather, the goal is to develop a healthy relationship with money and attain material autonomy and security, however you define it. A billionaire may never have a moment's rest, always thinking they don't have enough, and a homesteader living off the land may feel rich with a bountiful harvest. Your emotional well-being is more about your perception of money and security, rather than the attainment of a particular sum.

169

DECODING YOUR MOON'S HOUSE

➤ What stories do you have around money? How can you disentangle yourself from negative, limiting, or fearful money narratives?

➤ What regular personal finance activities can serve as self-care for you?

➤ What does financial and material security look like to you and how can you create a practical plan to achieve it?

MOON IN THE 3RD HOUSE

EMOTIONAL FULFILLMENT THROUGH COMMUNICATION, SUCH AS WRITING, SPEAKING, TEACHING, AND/OR ARTISTIC EXPRESSION

The **3RD HOUSE** is the place of communication in our charts. With your Moon placed here, you find emotional fulfillment and well-being through the exchange of ideas, especially through communicating about your emotions. If your 3rd House is a water sign, you may often communicate your emotions nonverbally and perceive other's emotions intuitively and empathetically. But for the most part, having your Moon in the 3rd House means that verbal communication about emotions will be essential for you to feel secure and satisfied. Look to the sign of your 3rd House for information about your style of communication (see chapter 5 for more about your Moon sign).

Beyond communicating about your emotions, having your Moon in the 3rd House speaks to a joy for communication and learning in general. It feels good to chat, connect, and share in the style of your Moon sign. In terms of your life's purpose, engaging activities that feed your desire for intellectual stimulation and sharing will help you to find that sense of flow.

DECODING YOUR MOON'S HOUSE

➤ How do you typically communicate about your emotions? What is your communication style (see your Moon sign in chapter 5)?

➤ How can you improve your approach to communication to feel more secure and satisfied in your relationships?

➤ What topics do you most enjoy studying and communicating about? What communication outlets are most engaging to you (e.g., talking one-on-one, podcasting, creating videos, writing, public speaking, teaching)? How can you bring more of your preferred kinds of communication into your personal and professional life?

MOON IN THE 4TH HOUSE

EMOTIONAL FULFILLMENT THROUGH CULTIVATING YOUR HOME AND FAMILY

The **4TH HOUSE** is the place of home and family in our charts. To have your Moon here indicates that you attain emotional fulfillment in your home and family. In the most basic sense, you achieve rest and restoration in your home. The kind of home that you seek to cultivate is described by your Moon sign (see chapter 5). Your familial connections are central to your life and sense of well-being. Know that family can be defined in whatever way is most supportive and meaningful to you, whether that is blood relatives or chosen family.

Beyond your physical home and immediate family, the 4th House also corresponds to your ancestry. You may feel called to connect with your cultural heritage and find satisfaction in understanding where you came from. The 4th House is the most private place in our chart, the safe haven we cultivate outside of the public eye. Your emotional well-being requires some reclusion to recharge from the exertion of life.

In terms of your life's purpose, this placement may simply mean you need to create enough time with home and family to recharge from your public and professional life. You may find deeper purpose in the home as a stay-at-home parent. Alternatively, you may find fulfillment in roles that help others create a sense of home and family, such as a social worker, adoption coordinator, or interior designer.

171

DECODING YOUR MOON'S HOUSE

➤ Looking at your Moon sign (chapter 5), what style of home and family do you need to create to feel emotionally fulfilled?

➤ In what ways is your home the place where you find emotional balance? If there are aspects of your home or family life that don't support your emotional well-being, how can those aspects be addressed?

➤ What is your relationship to your ancestors and culture? How do you find emotional fulfillment and comfort by connecting with your roots?

MOON IN THE 5TH HOUSE

EMOTIONAL FULFILLMENT THROUGH YOUR CREATIVE PURSUITS, RAISING YOUR CHILDREN, AND/OR WORKING WITH CHILDREN

The **5TH HOUSE** is the place of creativity and children. To have your Moon here indicates that you'll find emotional fulfillment through your creative work, raising your own children, or perhaps working with children (e.g., as a teacher or caregiver). The nature of your creativity is described by your Moon sign (see chapter 5), which can help you understand what kinds of creative work you'll be most fulfilled doing. Generally, if your 5th House element is earth, you'll be interested in creating tangible projects and engaging in tactile, perhaps practical crafts. Air signs in the 5th House are more concerned with creative projects that engage the mind, allow an exchange of ideas, and satisfy your curiosity. Water signs in the 5th House are interested in creative work that examines or evokes deep emotions. Fire signs in the 5th House are interested in projects that channel passion and are an expression of individual freedom. Figuring out what creative outlets are most nourishing to you will be key for your emotional health and living out your life's purpose.

With regard to children, your Moon in the 5th House means that you find emotional fulfillment in engagement with and caretaking of children. Parenting, teaching, caregiving, or child advocacy could all be satisfying for your emotional well-being and for supporting an overall sense of purpose in your life.

DECODING YOUR MOON'S HOUSE

➤ Considering your 5th House sign (see chapter 5), what types of creative projects call to you?

➤ What role do children play in your life? How does connecting with or caring for children factor into living a purposeful life?

➤ How does engaging in this creative work help you maintain emotional equilibrium?

MOON IN THE 6TH HOUSE

EMOTIONAL FULFILLMENT THROUGH CULTIVATING NOURISHING, PRODUCTIVE DAILY ROUTINES AND HABITS

The **6TH HOUSE** is the place of daily work and routines. It's how you organize and live out your life. Having your Moon in the 6th House means that you find emotional fulfillment in the day-to-day. Daily routines that feel nourishing and supportive will be essential for your well-being. Look to your Moon sign (chapter 5) for information about the style of daily schedule that will be most aligned for you. Your professional life will also likely be essential to your life's purpose and your sense of emotional satisfaction. While the 10th House describes your overall career and legacy, the 6th House corresponds to the work you do every day. You have a deeply felt heart's desire to engage in meaningful work. You don't just want to work for the weekend. You would benefit from finding a job that is satisfying every day and connects to long-term, meaningful goals. See part IV of this book for more on what your 6th House indicates and how to find purposeful work.

173

DECODING YOUR MOON'S HOUSE

➤ Considering your Moon sign (chapter 5), what kinds of daily rituals and habits best support your mental and physical well-being?

➤ Considering your Moon sign, what style of daily work and professional routines feels most fulfilling?

➤ How do your day-to-day tasks and routines connect with a larger sense of purpose in your life? Do they support long-term goals or connect with your ideals?

MOON IN THE 7TH HOUSE

EMOTIONAL FULFILLMENT THROUGH MEANINGFUL, COMMITTED PARTNERSHIP

The **7TH HOUSE** is the place of committed partnership, including romantic, platonic, and business partnerships. To have your Moon here means that you find emotional fulfillment in connecting one-on-one with your committed partners. Your romantic relationships and long-term, platonic friendships are critical to your well-being. If you have a business partner or work with clients, you may also feel that these relationships are emotionally satisfying. Essentially, you want to form deep, meaningful bonds with other people.

Having your Moon in the 7th House doesn't mean you're automatically adept at fostering healthy relationships, though. You would benefit from dedicating time to study the qualities and strategies of healthy relationships. How do you communicate your needs to your partners and make them feel safe to share their needs? How do you construct healthy boundaries? What do constructive conflict and resolution look like? Because committed partnership is so key to your emotional well-being, it would be wise to cultivate several close relationships. A tendency of this placement is to put all of your emotional eggs in one basket—usually a romantic partner or best friends—but that is a lot of pressure to put on one relationship. Creating an intimate network of meaningful relationships will support your well-being and alleviate overreliance on any one relationship.

174

DECODING YOUR MOON'S HOUSE

➤ Which committed partnerships are most supportive of your emotional well-being? What care and cultivation do these relationships require to be healthy and nurturing for you and your partners?

➤ What skills can you develop that will support healthy partnerships? Improving communication? Learning more about your attachment style?

➤ How do your committed partnerships bring a sense of purpose to your life? How can you honor the critical role these relationships play in your life? Can you prioritize them? How can you convey gratitude to your partners for the value and meaning they bring to your life?

MOON IN THE 8TH HOUSE

EMOTIONAL FULFILLMENT THROUGH TRANSFORMATIONAL EXPERIENCES AND TENDING TO YOUR MENTAL HEALTH

The **8TH HOUSE** is a complex place in the birth chart, covering several seemingly disparate topics. Not every signification of this house will resonate, so read through this description and take what resonates.

When thinking about the Moon being placed here, the first consideration is to reflect on the concept of endings, transformations, and new beginnings. You may be drawn to topics of endings, death, grief, as well as transformation and renewal. Another topic of life related to the 8th House is mental health and people with their Moon in the 8th House may be called to engage with mental health topics, perhaps by working in the mental health profession or creating art grappling with this topic. The through line with this placement is that engaging with the emotional depth and intensity of topics often deemed taboo might be deeply gratifying to you. Your life's purpose may be to facilitate others in excavating these topics, perhaps as an artist or psychologist.

The 8th House is also the place of the money and resources you owe to or share with others (e.g., loans, taxes, shared assets or bank accounts). Resources can also include time and emotional energy. To have the Moon in the 8th could indicate that your emotional well-being is concerned with the balance of how you share and collaborate with others, especially people you are financially bound to. On the one hand, sharing resources (time, money, emotional bandwidth) with your partner or loved ones could be a place of emotional support for you. Finding that balance with others provides security and peace. In a broader sense, this placement could point to your life's purpose involving the management of other people's money and assets, perhaps as a financial advisor or literary agent.

In terms of your emotional well-being, this placement may call you to tend to your own mental health. Look to the sign of your 8th House (chapter 5) for information about how you are emotionally activated and regulated, and for strategies on how best to find emotional equilibrium.

175

DECODING YOUR MOON'S HOUSE

➤ How do you engage with topics of death, transformation, and rebirth, personally or professionally? How is this work fulfilling to you?

➤ How does sharing resources with others provide you security and support?

➤ Does managing the resources of others play a major role in your life? In what way does this give your life purpose?

MOON IN THE 9TH HOUSE

EMOTIONAL FULFILLMENT THROUGH TRAVELING, LEARNING, AND TEACHING

––––––––––

The **9TH HOUSE** is the place of learning and philosophy. It is the part of our lives where we seek out truth and establish our beliefs. There are many roads to metaphysical understanding: formal study at university, independent research, traveling to experience new places and cultures, or spiritual study and practice to encounter divine wisdom. It is in these activities that your 9th House Moon finds replenishment and rest.

In terms of your life's purpose, you may feel called to a life of learning. Look to your Moon sign (chapter 5) for information on what it is you might feel called to learn or the method of study. Beyond inquiry, you may also be called to discuss and teach the wisdom you accrue as a teacher, author, speaker, or artist. There is a call to adventure in the 9th House, so you may feel drawn to distant shores and new experiences. Finding time to engage in learning, teaching, philosophy, and spirituality will help you maintain emotional equilibrium.

176

DECODING YOUR MOON'S HOUSE

➤ What topics of study are the most emotionally satisfying for you? What truths are you seeking? What travels are you called to embark on in service of answering your big questions?

➤ What spiritual practices are the most nourishing to you?

➤ In terms of your life's purpose, what do you feel called to learn or teach?

MOON IN THE 10TH HOUSE

EMOTIONAL FULFILLMENT THROUGH BUILDING
YOUR CAREER AND LEGACY

———

The **10TH HOUSE** is the place of career and public life. To have your Moon placed here calls you into the public eye. Look to your Moon sign (chapter 5) for information as to how you wish to be in your public life. For example, an individual with a 10th House Moon in Leo may feel compelled to self-expression and performance as an actor or musician. An individual with a 10th House Moon in Virgo, however, may be content with a less public stage, preferring a career of service to others in the medical profession. In part IV, you can learn more about your 10th House sign and the nature of your career.

It is in cultivating your career that you find fulfillment. This isn't to say that other aspects of your life aren't important, but rather that work plays a particularly central role in giving your life meaning. This isn't true for everyone and there can be some judgment from others who might find your dedication to work excessive. But this is your nature—to find satisfaction in your work. How can you embrace that in a way that is healthy and doesn't overly isolate or tax you?

DECODING YOUR MOON'S HOUSE

➤ Considering your 10th House sign (part IV), what style of career or public life are you called to? How does that already show up in your work or in your idealized work situation? In what ways is it emotionally fulfilling?

➤ How do you define work-life balance? How can this balance be revitalizing and satisfying?

➤ What body of work or legacy do you want to build?

MOON IN THE 11TH HOUSE

EMOTIONAL FULFILLMENT THROUGH SPENDING TIME WITH FRIENDS, BUILDING COMMUNITY, AND/OR CULTIVATING CLIENTS AND PATRONS

The **11TH HOUSE** is the place of friends, communities, patrons, clients, and fans. It's the place where people come together. To have your Moon in the 11th House indicates that your emotional well-being is cultivated in groups of people. It may be that your friend groups are essential to refilling your emotional cup. Perhaps it is performing before an audience of people that you feel most satisfied. Or perhaps it's advocating on behalf of a particular group of people that you find emotional fulfillment. Still others with this placement may feel called to build community, perhaps as an activist or in a profession with a client list. Any or all of these could be true for you. The essential through line is being in connection and community with the people who matter most to you.

Considering the element of your 11th House will give insight into how you want to engage with community and how that influences your emotional well-being. Generally, if your 11th House element is earth, you'll be interested in grounded, substantive relationships within your communities. Air signs here are more concerned with communities that allow for the exchange of ideas and intellectual connection. Water signs in the 11th House are interested in interpersonal connections that foster intimacy and allow for emotional depth. Fire signs in the 11th House seek communities of action, passion, and adventure. Figuring out what communities are most nourishing to you will be key for your emotional health and living out your life's purpose.

DECODING YOUR MOON'S HOUSE

➤ What groups of people are most important to you?

➤ What communities do you want to build?

➤ Considering your Moon sign (chapter 5), how do you engage with your communities and how is that emotionally satisfying for you?

MOON IN THE 12TH HOUSE

EMOTIONAL FULFILLMENT THROUGH PERSONAL INTROSPECTION AND/OR SPIRITUAL EXPERIENCES

The **12TH HOUSE** is the place of hidden things, from your secret projects to your unconscious mind to the unseen world of spirit and divine wisdom. To have your Moon in the 12th House indicates that you seek emotional security and replenishment in solitude. Having ample time alone for reflection or personal projects will be emotionally soothing for you.

You may also feel called to dig into unseen places for the wisdom hidden there. Psychological introspection, meditation, spiritual rituals, psychic channeling, dream interpretation—any method that seeks to draw out understanding from another realm is indicated by the Moon in the 12th House.

For some, the call to hidden places is much more literal. You may be called to work with incarcerated people, or people otherwise confined, perhaps in the hospital. You may be interested in things hidden from the eye and find solace in particle physics. Whether physical or metaphysical, you want to see what others cannot or choose not to.

The 12th House is also known as the place of personal undoing. If the 1st House is the place of self and where we construct ourselves, the 12th House is where we shed the container of identity. The Moon in the 12th House seeks to dissolve the ego and the illusion of separation to feel a sense of oneness and transcendence. How do you get out of your own head? What activities help your mind to stop so that you can be fully present in the moment? What activities evoke a sense of sublime awe?

179

DECODING YOUR MOON'S HOUSE

➤ What spiritual or psychological practices allow you to connect with your unconscious mind?

➤ What hidden things or places call to you? What do you want to uncover?

➤ How does solitude factor into your self-care? Can you make space to be alone and look within?

DECODING THE STARS

EMILY BRONTË

BIRTH DATE: July 30, 1818

BIRTH TIME: 2:49 p.m.

BIRTH LOCATION: Thornton, England

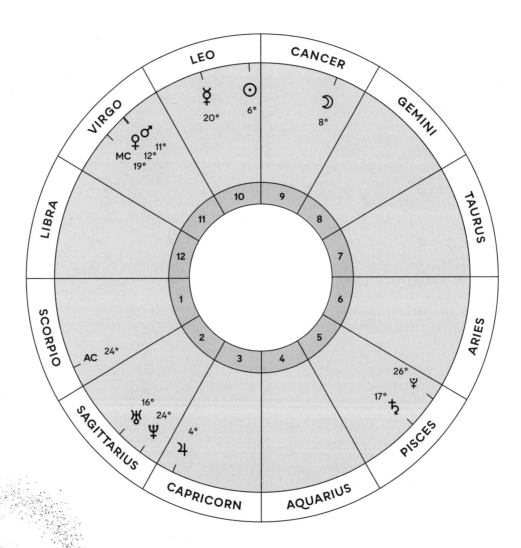

EMILY BRONTË was an English author made famous by her only novel, *Wuthering Heights*. In her personal life, she was a noted recluse. Her novel also stayed close to the topics of home and family, though with a decidedly Gothic flair. In looking at her chart, we can see indications of these attributes and how they coalesced in her life's purpose as an author.

Cancer is the sign of family and home, and individuals with their Moon in Cancer often find emotional security and fulfillment within these domains. Brontë was a noted homebody, apparently only leaving home to visit church and wander the moors where she lived. Her few attempts at long-distance travel were ultimately disliked and quickly abandoned. The 9th House is the place of long-distance travel, so having her Moon there might indicate a need to venture abroad, but because the 9th House sign is Cancer, the scope of 9th House travel is narrowed to the home. It is at home that, according to her sister Charlotte, Brontë felt the freedom necessary for her well-being.

The 9th House is also the place of studying, writing, and publishing. Having her Moon here indicates a relationship between Brontë's emotional well-being and her creative work. Brontë wrote original stories and poetry from a young age, often as a collaborative effort with her sister Anne (writing with family perhaps indicating a further expression of Cancer in the 9th House). Emily Brontë's Sun is in Leo in the 10th House of career, meaning that her life's purpose is centered on self-expression through her public life. Balancing her Sun's desire to shine through her creative work with her Moon's call to privacy and homelife, Brontë's ultimate legacy was as an author obscured by a pseudonym, only coming to prominence after her death. This isn't to say that these aspects of her chart indicate early death or posthumous fame, but rather that they indicate fame and a desire to stay out of the public eye. She died only a year after her novel was published, but had she lived longer, she likely would have continued her reclusive lifestyle despite rising acclaim.

The themes of her novel are both Cancerian (focused on home and family) and Scorpionic, motivated by her Scorpio Rising. *Wuthering Heights* is a tale of familial power struggles, forbidden love, and classism. It features numerous Gothic elements like physical and emotional brutality, vengeance, death, mental anguish, and hauntings. *Wuthering Heights* brings together Brontë's Scorpionic preoccupations with the macabre, blended with her Cancerian 9th House Moon's focus on home and family in her writing, as a way to self-express publicly her 10th House Leo Sun. Emily Brontë lived according to her true nature and the product of her authentic life continues to be acclaimed today.

CRACKING THE CODE
YOUR EMOTIONAL WELL-BEING

YOUR MOON SIGN + HOUSE

What aspects of your Moon sign description resonate with you?
How does your Moon sign help you understand the nature of your emotions?

What topics of life connected to your Moon house feel important to your emotional well-being?

Considering your Moon sign and house, what strategies would most help
you maintain emotional equilibrium?

YOUR MOON + YOUR SUN + RISING

Looking at your Sun sign and Moon sign, in what ways does your core nature complement and support your emotional well-being? In what ways do they conflict?

How does your life's primary motivation (your Rising sign) relate to and blend with your emotional needs (Moon sign)? In what ways do they work together and how do they conflict?

Look at your Sun, Moon, and Rising sign elements. Are they all in the same element, just two elements, or three different elements? How does this elemental mix manifest in your approach to the world (review the meanings of the elements in chapters 1 and 3)?

Considering your Sun, Moon, and Rising sign ruler houses, what areas of life are most important for you? How do these areas of life intersect in meaningful ways for you? Where do you find flow when blending these house topics?

183

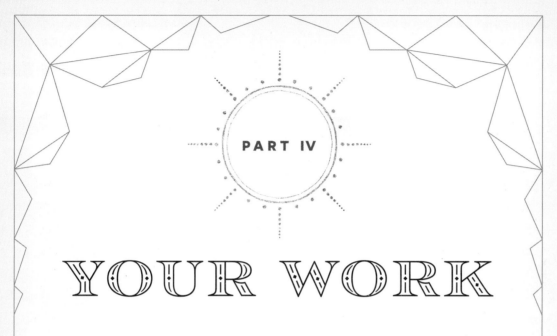

PART IV

YOUR WORK

FINDING YOUR LIFE'S PURPOSE IS, on the most essential level, about coming to understand yourself—wholly and unapologetically—and living as an expression of your authentic self. I hope, in reading these chapters and reflecting on your chart, that you see your life's purpose is as much about being yourself as doing any particular job or activity. That being said, we do live in a material world and all of us are, in our own ways, creative, curious, and productive. We feel driven to engage in hobbies and, for most of us, we have to work for a living. How does your life's purpose connect with your career? What does your birth chart say about the kinds of work that will be most fulfilling to you? In this part, we'll dig into what your birth chart has to say about how you make money, how you prefer to work, and the nature of your vocation.

You'll notice that part IV is organized differently than the previous sections. For most of the book so far, we've focused on a specific luminary or planet: the Sun, your Rising sign ruler, and the Moon. In this section, we'll be looking at three houses—the 2nd, 6th, and 10th Houses—that together describe your approach to money and work, collectively referred to as the Houses of Substance. Your Houses of Substance will always be in the same element, creating a consistent energic theme for how you approach your work life. Part IV begins with chapter 7, **Your Houses of Substance**, giving you an overview of these three houses and the significance of their element. Chapters 8 through 11 then dive deep into your Houses of Substance by element and sign.

7

Your Houses of Substance

As we've already discussed, understanding your Sun, Rising, and Moon placements gives you insight into the kinds of work that aligns with your true nature. Your Sun placement helps you see which activities energize you and your core self that wants to be expressed. Your Rising sign gives insights into what motivates you and should help you identify the kinds of work that tap into that motivation. Your Moon sign explains what you need in order to feel emotionally secure and satisfied, which can help narrow down the kinds of work and workplace environments that will feel most nourishing to you.

But your birth chart has more to say about your work life. In fact, three of the twelve houses in your birth chart deal directly with your work: the 2nd, 6th, and 10th Houses. These houses are sometimes referred to as the Houses of Substance, in that they deal with the materially sustaining aspects of your life:

> **2ND HOUSE:** The skills with which you make money and how you manage your money and assets

➤ **6TH HOUSE:** Your day-to-day work and habits

➤ **10TH HOUSE:** Your career, vocation, and public life

Part IV will walk you through your Houses of Substance, giving you insights into your relationship with money, work skills, habits, and the kind of career you're drawn to build.

The Element of Your Houses of Substance

Before digging into the signs that occupy these three houses in your chart, you'll first want to consider their **element**. When using the Whole Sign Houses system, the Houses of Substance are always the same element (see **Understanding the Code** for a refresher on house systems). So, if your 2nd House is an earth sign, then your 6th and 10th Houses will also be earth signs. If your 2nd House is a fire sign, then your 6th and 10th Houses will also be fire signs, and so on. This means that there is a consistent, elemental energy about how you relate to money and work.

▽ **EARTH** Your approach to work is pragmatic, structured, and goal-oriented.

△ **AIR** Your approach to work is communicative, cerebral, and inquisitive.

▽ **WATER** Your approach to work is relational, intuitive, and emotionally intelligent.

△ **FIRE** Your approach to work is passionate, adventurous, and action-oriented.

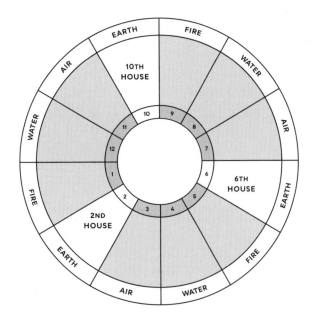

YOUR HOUSES OF SUBSTANCE

After getting to know the element of your Houses of Substance and how that generally informs your approach to money and work, we'll then look at how each sign imbues a different style to the topics of the house it occupies. Your Houses of Substance may all be earth, but what does it mean to have a Taurus 2nd House versus a Capricorn 2nd House?

Your Houses of Substance and the Rest of Your Chart

When reading the descriptions for your Houses of Substance, some may ring immediately true and some may feel like they don't sit right or even rub you the wrong way. The reason for this has to do with which signs and elements your planets and luminaries fall in. While you have all twelve zodiacal signs in your chart, there are only eight planets (Mercury, Venus, Mars, Jupiter, Saturn, Uranus, Neptune, and Pluto) and two luminaries (Sun and Moon), so it is guaranteed that you will have at least two signs (and therefore two houses) that have no planets or luminaries in it. The signs and elements where the planets and luminaries are placed color your nature. We've discussed the Sun, Moon, and the importance of the Ascendant point and your Rising sign, but the other planets provide additional information about your nature as well. Often, the placement of planets and luminaries will be weighted to a few signs or a couple of elements, whereas other signs and elements will have no planets or luminaries. You will feel an affinity to the qualities of the signs and elements more weighted in your chart, and may struggle to connect with the qualities of elements and signs not weighted in your chart. Even so, all the signs and elements are part of you and important in understanding how you relate to the world.

How does this influence your relationship to your Houses of Substance? The element and signs of your Houses of Substance describe your best strategies for success with money and work. If you have planets or luminaries in your 2nd, 6th, or 10th Houses, you will likely have some affinity to the element of your Houses of Substance and more ease in employing those success strategies. In Example Chart 1, this individual has several planets and both luminaries in their Houses of Substance (Moon in Gemini in the 2nd House; Saturn, Jupiter, Pluto, the Sun, and Mercury in Libra in the 6th House). This person would connect strongly with the qualities of the air signs, so would likely be communicative, cerebral, and curious. These are the same essential qualities of their work and money success strategies. I would expect this person to be comfortable and adept in their work environment and for their work to be central to their life's purpose.

Conversely, for individuals with few or no planets in their Houses of Substance, they might not feel much affinity to the nature of that element. In Example Chart 2, the individual (born two hours later than the person in Example Chart 1) only has one planet in their Houses of Substance (Uranus in Scorpio in the 6th House). This person has many planets in air signs and may struggle to relate to the watery nature of their Houses of Substance. Being weighted toward the air element could make this person cerebral and often stuck in their own head, whereas their Houses of Substance would mean that intuition, relationship building, and emotional intelligence are key strategies for

188

EXAMPLE CHART 1:
MANY PLANETS AND
LUMINARIES IN THE
HOUSES OF SUBSTANCE

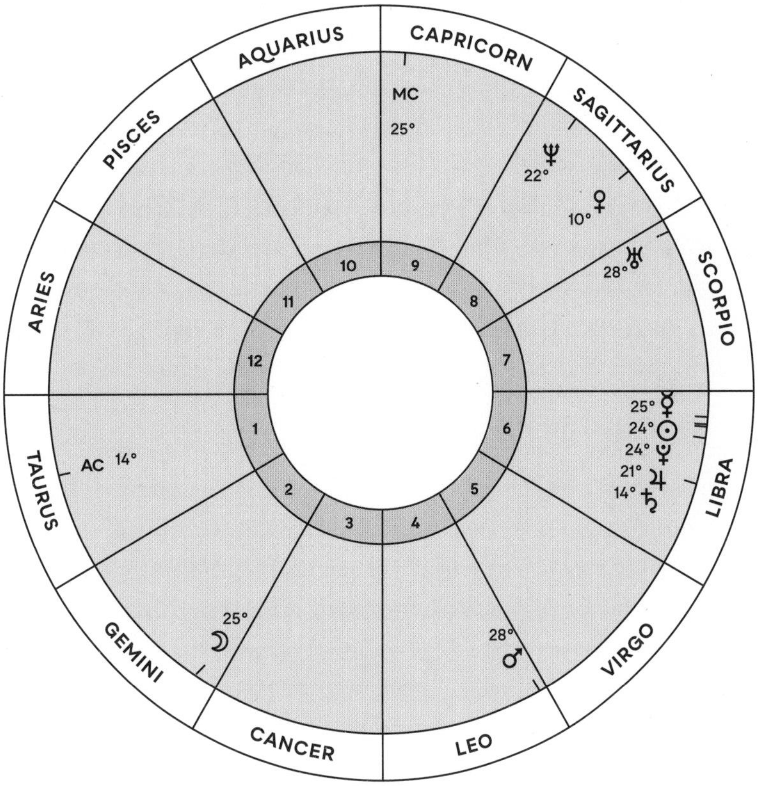

EXAMPLE CHART 2:
FEW PLANETS IN THE
HOUSES OF SUBSTANCE

YOUR HOUSES OF SUBSTANCE

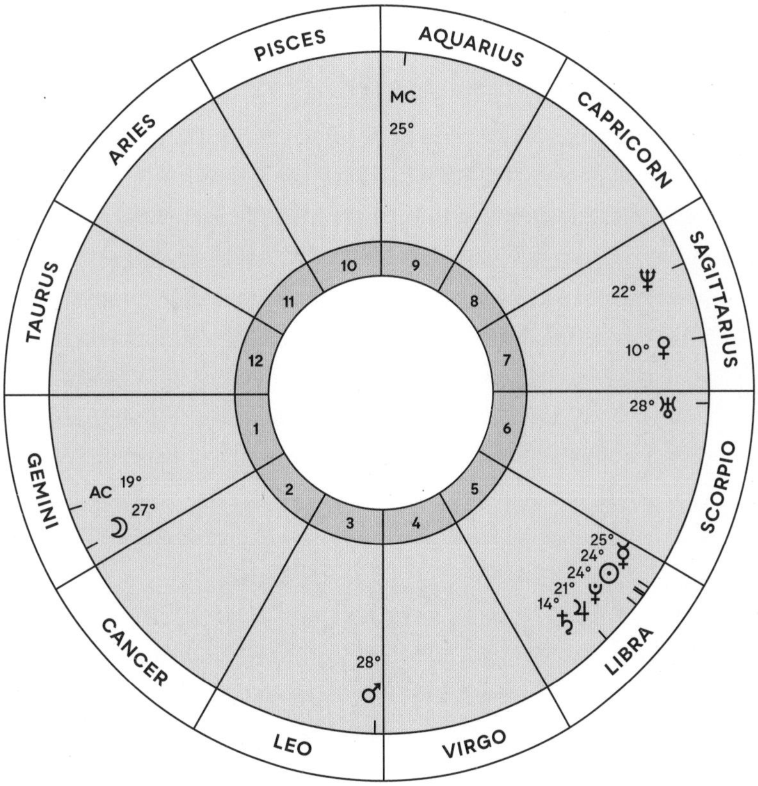

approaching work and money. This person would likely find that water elemental qualities would be essential in their work life, but perhaps they don't enjoy those elements as much as the air aspects of their work life.

Look at your own chart and see whether you have any planets or luminaries in your 2nd, 6th, or 10th Houses. Note the element of your Houses of Substance and read through your element's chapter, then answer the questions in **Cracking the Code: Your Work** to reflect on your best strategies for money and work.

Your Rising Sign

In addition to checking whether you have any planets or luminaries in your Houses of Substance, it's important to note that your Rising sign element will always be somewhat at odds with your Houses of Substance element. For example, if your Rising sign is a fire sign, you will always have earth signs for your Houses of Substance. Fire prioritizes action and passion, while earth prioritizes planning and persistent work over time. Recall from chapter 3 that the Rising sign speaks to what motivates you in this life. Having your motivation in a different element than how you approach money and work can sometimes feel conflicting. The wisdom that astrology encourages is to reflect on what motivates you (Rising sign) and how you work (Houses of Substance) and then find a synthesis of these two seemingly divergent energies.

The Midheaven

The Midheaven, or Medium Coeli (MC), is a calculated point that represents the highest point the Sun reached along the ecliptic on the day of your birth. The Midheaven provides information about our public life, career path, and reputation. In some house systems (e.g., Placidus), the Midheaven marks the start of the 10th House. In this book, we've been using the Whole Sign Houses system, which means the MC could fall in a house other than the 10th House. If your MC resides in your 10th House, then there is additional focus on the signification of your 10th House sign in terms of your career and legacy.

If your MC appears in a place other than the 10th House, the topics of that house are pulled into and blended with the career interpretation of your 10th House. For example, if your MC is in your 9th House, then topics of publishing, writing, teaching, higher education, travel, philosophy, or spirituality will be important to your career. See page 17 for a refresher on the meanings of the houses if your MC falls outside the 10th House.

YOUR HOUSES OF SUBSTANCE

Fill in the blanks with information from your own birth chart.

The element of your Houses of Substance: _____

Your 2nd House sign: _____

Your 6th House sign: _____

Your 10th House sign: _____

Your MC House: _____

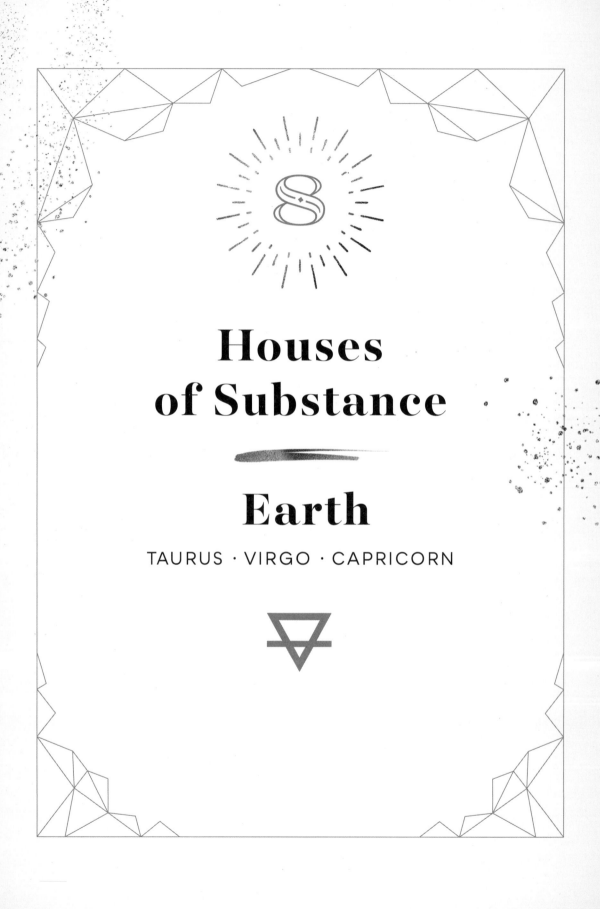

Houses
of Substance

Earth

TAURUS · VIRGO · CAPRICORN

EARTH AS THE ELEMENT of your Houses of Substance means that, financially and vocationally, you're concerned with building structures set on firm foundations that will last the test of time. When constructing a legacy, you cannot hurry. The best approach is methodical and slow. Whether you're building a financial nest egg, a business, or a bespoke artisan chair, you have a clear goal in mind and a pathway to achieve it. You aren't daunted by time or effort.

Your work is concerned with material outcomes. What is the tangible result from your labors? What have you created? More than other elements, you are interested in financial and career achievements that can be concretely evidenced—on a balance sheet, in an art gallery, at a farmers' market stall, in a quarterly shareholder report. You feel most in flow and successful at work when you see a clear connection between your effort and an outcome that is valuable to you.

If you have several planets or luminaries in earth signs, this description will likely ring true for you. The placement of planets in your Houses of Substance draws the focus of your life to your career and the earthy nature of these signs. You will more naturally approach organizing your money in a structured way, prefer habitual daily routines, and steadily build your career achievements over time.

However, if you do not have many planets or luminaries placed in these Houses of Substance, you may feel in conflict with the rigidity and long-term effort this earth energy requires. For example, a person with Sagittarius Rising and Gemini Sun with few or no planets in earth signs will feel motivated by action, curiosity, and change, while perhaps feeling chafed by a structured work life. But the nature of this person's professional skills, relationship to money, and career trajectory is earth. They are destined to align to the earthy style of their Houses of Substance and will benefit from connecting with this part of their true nature.

How can you align with the earthy nature of your Houses of Substance, especially if you don't have many planets in earth signs and feel disconnected from these approaches? Read through the description of your 2nd, 6th, and 10th House signs. See how they resonate with you. What feels like a nourishing, supportive approach and what about those descriptions gets your hackles up? If you struggle with creating the structure and discipline the earth signs of these houses signify, can you seek support? Could you work with your boss to set clearer goals, download a budgeting app, or meet with a career coach? External accountability can be particularly helpful for those with earth in their Houses of Substance and those with few earth placements generally. After reading the descriptions for your signs, answer the questions in **Cracking the Code: Your Work** to reflect on how past work experiences have capitalized on your earthy work nature and how you can better align with this part of your nature in the future.

Your 2nd House

The 2nd House pertains to your money and assets, how you manage them, as well as the skills with which you make them. Having an earth sign in your 2nd House means that you are particularly concerned with the accumulation of monetary wealth (whereas other signs might be interested in less tangible assets). You approach managing your money in a methodical, structured way. You also employ the unique skills of your specific 2nd House earth sign in order to make money. Let's take a closer look at your specific 2nd House sign.

♉ TAURUS

The fixed earth sign, Taurus is the most stubborn and plodding of all the earth signs. Taurus will not be rushed. Taurus chooses a trajectory and commits wholeheartedly to that plan. You are satisfied with long-term investments, knowing that a small seed planted in spring will yield large returns come harvest. You perhaps prefer a mostly hands-off approach to investment, where you set the plan and let it run in the background, checking in to water, prune, and troubleshoot pests as your crop grows steadily.

Even with your penchant for consistent effort over time, and despite the Taurean aversion to risk or hasty action, you may still struggle to be responsible with your money. Taurus is a Venus-ruled sign that loves the pleasures that money can buy at least as much as, if not more than, the security that a steady income and healthy savings can provide. Be honest with yourself of any tendency toward untenable extravagance and seek to prioritize your financial well-being in a way that makes you feel safe as well as satisfied. How can you manage financial security as well as the indulgent pleasures that make life enjoyable?

In addition to your approach to personal finance, the 2nd House sign also describes skills you employ to earn money. Taurean skills are a tactile expression of Venusian qualities: art making, craftwork, building, and gardening—anything to do with manipulating physical materials into practical or aesthetically pleasing products or cultivating the natural world. Taurus is also associated with financial systems, and having Taurus in the 2nd House could correspond to working in finance.

♍ VIRGO

Virgo is ruled by Mercury, god of speedy travel and communication. There is a busy, cerebral energy to Virgo that, for you, is directed at your personal finances and how you make money. In terms of managing your money, Virgo in the 2nd House is about meticulous organization. Spreadsheets, calendar reminders for payments, savings goals, apps to track your spending—you love it all. You aren't passive about your finances; rather, you monitor your income, spending, and investments with a critical eye for improvement. Unless you have most of your planets and luminaries in fire or air signs, you'll likely be risk averse, more interested in managing what you can control rather than betting on volatile financial ventures.

The skills with which you make money include the Virgoan knack for perfection. You spot errors and opportunities for improvement. You're adept at quality control, editing, and giving constructive feedback. Virgo is also often correlated with the medical profession and other healing modalities, so you may feel called to work in that field. Virgo is also a sign dedicated to service to others, which may feature in how you make money.

♑ CAPRICORN

To have Capricorn in the 2nd House confers an approach to personal finance that is goal-oriented and likely traditional. Capricorn is driven to work diligently to summit new peaks. You'll feel in alignment when setting financial goals and achieving them. You'll likely appreciate jobs that have performance-related financial incentives and structured pay increases. You are motivated by achieving financial targets and feel a sense of accomplishment and control with each new achievement. If you have most of your planets in freewheeling signs like Gemini, Pisces, or Sagittarius, you may not resonate with this description. Even so, Capricorn is the nature of how you approach money most effectively. If Capricorn's rigidity feels foreign to you, you can seek out external accountability at work or with a financial coach who can help you structure financial and professional goals. You may find that being more regimented and goal-oriented in your finances feels more natural than you would have thought.

In terms of the skills with which you make money, Capricorn's primary professional skill is tenacity toward achievement. Your skill is that you get it done, whatever it is. Capricorn is a Saturn-ruled sign, and Saturn is the planet of rules and structure. Even if you're an unstructured, carefree Pisces Sun, having Capricorn in your 2nd House means you have some facility with creating pathways to desired outcomes (for yourself or, maybe, clients) and that this is a primary skill with which you make money.

Your 6th House

The 6th House pertains to your day-to-day work, daily schedules, and regular habits. Having an earth sign in your 6th House imbues those aspects of life with a grounded, steady energy. Let's take a closer look at your specific 6th House sign.

♉ TAURUS

While the other two earth signs tend to have a structured nature, Taurus is more like a wild verdant meadow than a manicured walled garden. In your daily rituals and day-to-day work, you're more interested in pleasure and beauty than organization and efficiency. Having a daily routine that prioritizes leisurely breakfasts or lunches, an aesthetically pleasing workspace, rest, listening to music, and taking things slowly will be most satisfying to you. Things will get done in your time, and not a moment sooner. If you have planets or luminaries in Capricorn or Virgo, you may have a greater affinity for structure and schedules, but if most of your planets fall in water, air, or fire signs, you're likely to have a more casual approach to your daily routine.

In what ways can you bring Venusian pleasure into your daily life? Consider decadent self-care rituals, beautifying your desk, or creating time for relaxation and beauty in your week. There can be a general judgment against pleasure and rest in our work life, as if it is antithetical to being productive and achieving your goals. But you know this is a falsehood left over from an antiquated industrial age. You see that rest and beauty support your work by nurturing your physical and mental health. In addition to daily work routines, the 6th House encompasses the habits that support your physical health. Quiet time, pleasure, and going at your own pace support your work as well as your physical well-being. Your imagination needs space for inspiration. Resist the rhetoric of the daily grind. Find your own pace.

♍ VIRGO

To have Virgo in your 6th House means your daily routines benefit from meticulous structure. You're always looking for ways to improve efficiency: organizing your time with a detailed calendar, utilizing productivity and scheduling apps, or automating rote tasks. Keen attention to detail in your everyday habits—personal and professional—will pay major dividends, so it's worth the effort to set up productivity systems and regularly assess the efficacy of your methods.

Virgo is also a sign associated with service to others and specifically the medical profession, so you may find that jobs where you routinely help others, especially through healing modalities, will be most satisfying. In addition to daily work routines, the 6th House encompasses your day-to-day personal health rituals. Given Virgo's affinity for physical well-being and care, attention to your health routines will be especially important. Make sure that your daily routine includes healthy habits for your body and mind. Virgo is a busy, industrious sign and you may tend to run yourself ragged. For you, what gets tracked gets done, so add self-care to your schedule.

♑ CAPRICORN

To have Capricorn in your 6th House means that your daily work and routines benefit from being achievement-focused. What are you accomplishing today and how is it a step closer to your goal? Saturn, the ruler of Capricorn, is concerned with structure, and so it may be most essential just to have set routines, but you may find yourself most productive if you can tie your daily work and rituals to long-term achievements. Professionally, it's helpful to think about how your day-to-day work supports the overall career you're seeking to build (look to your 10th House for more on this). Capricorn 6th House reminds us that it's the actions that we take every day that culminate in our long-term accomplishments. What really matters to you in the long term (professionally or otherwise)? How do your day-to-day routines help or hinder those long-term goals?

In addition to work routines, the 6th House also speaks to our health and the daily rituals that support our physical well-being. Structured health regimes and setting health goals for yourself may be particularly fruitful for you.

Your 10th House

Whereas your 2nd House talks about work skills and the 6th House describes your daily work, the 10th House sign describes the nature of your overall career and public life. What is the legacy you're building? How are you cultivating the work and image you present to the world? Having an earth sign in your 10th House generally confers a concern with tangible, measurable outcomes for your career. You want to build or grow something. Let's take a closer look at your specific 10th House sign.

♉ TAURUS

Taurus in your 10th House colors your career with a rosy Venusian tint. Beauty, pleasure, the natural world, art, craftsmanship—these are the purview of Taurus. Does this mean you will have a career as a woodworker or a chef? Maybe. If you have planets or luminaries in your Taurus 10th House, you are more likely to be interested in a career that is about the pleasures of the five senses. More often, though, Taurus 10th House casts a Venusian tint to your overall career, whatever it may be. Consider your core nature (Sun sign), what motivates you (Rising sign), and the skills with which you make money (2nd House). Taken together, these significations help you understand what work you're here to do in the world. Add a dash of Taurean luxury, and what do you get?

All Taurus 10th House folks have Leo as their Rising sign (see chapter 3 for more on your Rising sign), which means you are motivated to authentically self-express and to be recognized and applauded for your skills and performance. How is your Leonine enthusiasm supported by your earthy Houses of Substance? How does your Taurus 10th House help you translate your Leo drive to self-express into a substantive body of work? With Leo Rising, your Sun is doubly important since it is also your Rising sign ruler (see chapter 4). When wondering how you are motivated to self-express, consider your Sun sign and house. What career do you want to build that is in alignment with the nature of your Sun placement? How do Taurean qualities help to ground and support the career and legacy you are building from your self-expression?

♍ VIRGO

Having Virgo in your 10th House speaks to a career dedicated to perfecting or improving. What you feel called to perfect is informed by your core nature (Sun sign). How do the skills and desires of your Sun sign blend with the Virgoan drive to evaluate and improve in your career? Virgo is associated with being of service to others and the healing modalities. In the case of healing professions, it's clear how the Virgoan skills of identifying ailments and knowing the perfect remedy prove potent. But you can help others improve outside of the medical profession, of course. Where do you feel called professionally to employ the practical, no-nonsense caregiving of Virgo?

All Virgo 10th House folks have Sagittarius as their Rising sign, which means you are motivated by the energy of Sagittarius (see chapter 3 for more on your Rising sign). Faith, optimism, and a desire to know and understand meaningful, universal truths is what gets you out of bed in the morning. Sagittarius is also a sign that is understanding and accepting of all people and paths, which is supportive of a Virgoan career path of service to others. How does your warmth and sense of adventure blend with the Virgoan drive to help and improve?

♑ CAPRICORN

Having Capricorn in the 10th House speaks to your professional legacy of achieving accomplishments and being publicly recognized for those achievements. Capricorn sets its sights on the summit, plots a path, and tenaciously hits the trail until the peak is reached. And there is always another, higher peak. Capricorn is generally a traditional sign, meaning that you may find yourself in a traditional career with a well-delineated advancement path, though if you have Uranus in your 1st or 10th House, or if it is the ruler of your Sun sign, you may march to the beat of your own drum.

Your Rising sign is Aries (see chapter 3), which means your motivation in life is to initiate action and fight for something. You can see how that drive supports the Capricorn nature of your career and public life. Aries energy gets you out of bed in the morning and Capricorn energy keeps your eye on the prize in terms of what you want to build in this life. Look to your Sun sign to see how your core nature gives insights about the types of work and achievements you want to engage in. Aries Rising and Capricorn 10th House could accomplish anything, if you put your mind to it. One drawback of Aries is not having enough commitment to stay the course long term. That's Capricorn's purview, but if you don't have many planets or luminaries in earth signs, you may find commitment to a path challenging. Second-guessing yourself or constantly changing course because you're bored can keep you from accomplishing any of your goals. What accountability and project management systems can help you stay committed to and progressing toward your career goals?

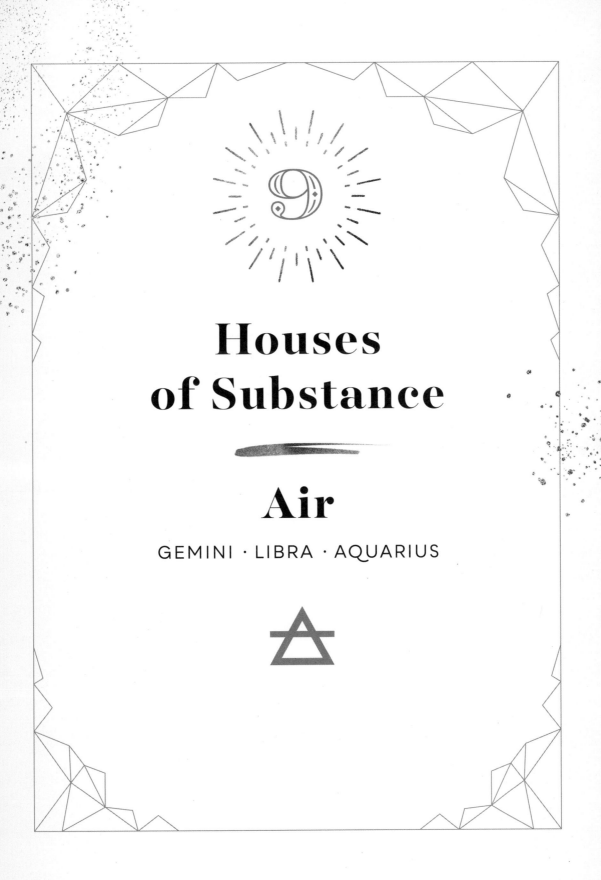

9

Houses of Substance

Air

GEMINI · LIBRA · AQUARIUS

AIR AS THE ELEMENT of your Houses of Substance means that you approach finances and work from a cerebral lens. Air commands the cool, cutting edge of logic and an inquisitive, problem-solving prowess. You find yourself in flow when your powers of mind are brought to bear on your work tasks. Work that foregrounds scheming, troubleshooting, learning, teaching, philosophizing, or investigating will elicit the best work from you. In the workplace, your mind demands stimulation or you'll easily become bored and unproductive.

In addition to cognitive ability, air signs are also adept at communication. In your work, you're able to both comprehend situations and concepts and share your thoughts effectively with others. Air usually has a strong bent toward language as the primary form of communication (e.g., speaking and writing), but you might find that you communicate best through visual or auditory means. Finding work that provides opportunities for you to collaborate, instruct, negotiate, or persuade will help fulfill the calling of your air sign Houses of Substance.

Overall, the nature of your work is the exchange of ideas, the development of new modes of thinking, or the devising of strategies. When looking to the Houses of Substance, you get a sense of what you value, and for those with air signs, there is a high value placed on intellectual rigor, sense-making, and communicating. You understand that everything humans have ever done began as an idea and it is in the creative crucible of the mind that new worlds will be formed.

This description will likely ring true for you if you have several planets or luminaries in air signs. The more planetary and luminary placements in air signs you have, the airier your nature. However, if you do not have many planets or luminaries placed in these Houses of Substance, you may feel in conflict with the communicative, intellectual energy that air requires. For example, a person with Capricorn Rising and an Aries Sun with few or no planets in air signs will feel motivated by structure and tangible results and have an innate drive to act, while perhaps feeling the intellectual pursuits of air signs to be too ephemeral. The person's fire Sun wants to do, not overthink. Their earth Rising wants a clear path to defined achievements, when air can be too freewheeling. But the nature of this person's professional skills, relationship to money, and career trajectory is air. They are destined to align with the airy style of their Houses of Substance and will benefit from connecting with this part of their true nature.

How can you align with the airy nature of your Houses of Substance, especially if you don't have many planets in air signs and feel disconnected from these approaches? Read through the descriptions of your 2nd, 6th, and 10th House signs. See how they resonate with you. What about them feels invigorating and what seems draining? After reading the descriptions for your signs, answer the questions in **Cracking the Code: Your Work** to reflect on how past work experiences have capitalized on your airy work nature and how you can better align with your nature in the future.

Your 2nd House

The 2nd House pertains to your money and assets, how you manage them, as well as the skills with which you make them. Having an air sign in your 2nd House means that you approach managing and making money through an intellectual lens. Money is an intellectual construct, after all, and you're adept at playing the chess game of commerce. Let's take a closer look at your specific 2nd House sign.

GEMINI

Gemini is a mutable sign, which is to say that it is a sign of change and transition. As an air sign, it has a sense of boundlessness, unstructured in its intellectual curiosity, skipping from one idea to the next. Ruled by Mercury, this is perhaps the airiest of the air signs, because Mercury is the planet overseeing thought and communication. Mercury is also known for speed, trickery, and duplicity (or perhaps multiplicity). All of these attributes become the skills with which you make money. This isn't to say you don't have many other excellent qualities that also contribute to your success at work, but it is these Gemini qualities that are your major revenue makers. Having a quick wit, being comfortable with change, trying things out, following ideas down the rabbit hole, having spirited discussions, and playing devil's advocate are your unique gifts that help you make money. You may also find that you have multiple revenue streams at once or that you shift through different careers more than your friends (who perhaps have earth or water Houses of Substance or a fixed sign in the 2nd House).

In terms of managing your money, you may have a somewhat cavalier approach to personal finance unless you have several planets in earth signs. Gemini is a speedy sign, so you could be spending money as quickly as you make it. If you find that your lack of structure isn't helping you achieve your financial goals, finding external accountability to ensure money is saved and spent according to plan (like direct deposits into savings or retirement accounts or budgeting apps) can be helpful.

LIBRA

Libra's symbol is the scales, illustrating the core quality of this Venus-ruled sign: balance. In the 2nd House, this skill of balance can manifest in several ways. It may be that you excel in aesthetic balance: interior design, graphic design and other visual arts, or fashion. As a Venus-ruled air sign, you are interested in the creation of beauty, but also in its intellectual and cultural trappings, so you may find yourself drawn to be an art historian or a gallery curator. Bringing the air sign's intellectual and communicative prowess to bear on the goal of balance, Libra in your 2nd House may manifest in your ability to mediate conflict and negotiate contracts or business deals. Do you find that you more often have jobs that require skills in aesthetic balance or interpersonal diplomacy?

AQUARIUS

Aquarius's traditional ruler is Saturn, the planet of structure and rules. Aquarius turns its mental prowess on understanding and refining systems. What are the philosophical underpinnings that prop up a given system? From testing the efficiency of your company's accounts payable processes to deconstructing the discourse on the military-industrial complex, you're adept at seeing the big picture, breaking it down into its constituent parts, and testing the logic of each facet. You aren't hampered by ties to tradition, though, like your Saturnian sibling sign, Capricorn. Aquarius's modern ruler, Uranus, is the planet of rebellion, revolution, and innovation. You use your intellectual skill and distance to evaluate processes and philosophies with an eye for radical improvement. You're not afraid of championing audacious change, if the data supports that course of action. Neither are you so idealistic that you ignore the need to structure realistic, often incremental changes to attain the overall goal. Systems thinking, dispassionate insight, and innovative problem-solving serve as your key money-making skills.

Your 6th House

The 6th House pertains to your day-to-day work, daily schedules, and regular habits. It also relates to your personal health, which is, in part, a result of your daily habits. Having an air sign in your 6th House brings an intellectual, inquisitive, and communicative approach to how you live out your day-to-day life. Each air sign imparts its unique signature on the topics of this house. Let's take a closer look at your specific 6th House sign.

GEMINI

Gemini in your 6th House demands novelty and intellectual stimulation in your daily work schedule. It isn't that you can't stand routine, as long as there is enough challenging, interesting work to keep your busy mind engaged. You want opportunities to follow your interests and talk about ideas. An environment that allows for play, debate, or endless research would appeal to you.

In terms of personal health habits and your daily routines, you may be more interested in the research than the results. You'll try any morning routine once or lose hours researching supplements: anything that sparks your curiosity and gets the mental gears turning. Keeping your routine fresh and interesting may be a helpful approach for successful healthy habits.

LIBRA

Libra in your 6th House desires harmony, balance, and beauty in your day-to-day work and habits. When Libra is in your 6th House, that means Taurus is your Rising sign, so your key life motivation (Rising sign) and how you live your day-to-day life (6th House) are both Venus-ruled signs. Beauty, pleasure, and balance are central to who you are and how you live your life. Lean into the Venusian vibes that call to you. Aesthetics are not frivolous; they are essential. Libra in your 6th House can also manifest in your life through acting as the peacemaker at work. Mediation or diplomacy could be a formal part of your job description or an informal role you take on. Your ability to see all sides of a situation and bring the team to an agreeable compromise could be particularly satisfying.

In terms of personal health habits and your daily routines, you may find that sumptuous personal care and health rituals will be most supportive to your physical well-being. Trying to maintain balance in all aspects of health should be prioritized, including a balance between work and pleasure. Attempting to adhere to strict regimes will likely prove futile and unfulfilling.

AQUARIUS

Aquarius in your 6th House brings Saturnian order and Uranian innovation to your day-to-day work and personal habits. You may always be looking for the latest productivity hack or an app to improve efficiency. You may have a marked desire for freedom and autonomy, leading you to avoid micromanaging bosses or jobs shackled to rigid, antiquated systems. You want to have influence over regular improvements in how your job functions, which could require simply that you have a supportive, communicative relationship with your boss, or you may need greater control as a freelancer or an entrepreneur. Aquarius is also a sign associated with supporting communities and humanitarian efforts generally, so you may find that working with groups or in support of community action initiatives is most fulfilling to you.

In terms of personal health habits and your daily routines, you may find that a strict structure is most supportive to your physical well-being. Constantly evaluating the efficacy of your habits and making tweaks and innovations will be a valuable approach for you.

Your 10th House

Whereas your 2nd House talks about work skills and the 6th House describes your daily work, the 10th House sign describes the nature of your overall career and public life. What is the legacy you're building? How are you cultivating the work and image you present to the world? Having an air sign in your 10th House is about creating a body of work that is the culmination of your intellectual expertise. Each air sign imparts its unique style to your career. Let's take a closer look at your specific 10th House sign.

GEMINI

With Gemini in your 10th House, your legacy is a portfolio of your brilliance. Gemini has a multiplicity of interests, and your curiosity and ability to synthesize disparate ideas from various domains guarantee that you will be unique in whatever professional fields you occupy. Gemini in the 10th House, and air signs for your Houses of Substance generally, require that you find work that centers your intellectual ability. Allow yourself to be curious and not held back by limiting, antiquated approaches to career that prioritize adherence to a rigid pathway, allegiance to one company, or the fallacy that how things have always been done is how they should be done. Your career will be a collection of the triumphs of your unique and magnificent mind.

All Gemini 10th House folks have Virgo as their Rising sign. This means that you are motivated in life by a mutable, Mercury-ruled sign (Virgo Rising) and that your career and life's work is also colored by a mutable, Mercury-ruled sign (Gemini 10th House). Your Virgo Rising brings structure, discernment, and organization to the wily whims of your Gemini career. Virgo Rising is motivated to perfect and be of service to others and Gemini 10th House wants to think, problem-solve, and communicate. How do these significations show up for you? How do they blend with your core nature (Sun sign)?

LIBRA

To have Libra in your 10th House means you're building a legacy of balance. Libra brings harmony to the world through aesthetic beauty or interpersonal peacemaking. It is likely that one side of these Libran scales calls to you. If you feel pulled to the aesthetic side, you may find career fulfillment in the creation of art, beautiful and harmonious spaces, music, fashion, or events. Libra is a sign of culture and refinement, so your career may have you contributing to or curating intellectual and material culture. Alternatively, you may feel called toward the diplomacy side of Libra, brokering peace between people, be it as a human resources representative or a delegate to the United Nations.

All Libra 10th House folks have Capricorn as their Rising sign. That means that you are motivated in life by Capricorn energy (see chapter 3). Both Capricorn and Libra are cardinal signs, which means your motivation in life and your career are marked by a call to initiate and lead. Your Capricorn Rising motivates you to achieve and create tangible results. Your Libra 10th House energy could manifest as a leader adept at facilitating peaceful, equitable, productive work environments. Or perhaps more to the aesthetic side of things, your Capricorn drive to create and achieve will help you produce a Venusian body of work, however you engage with art and beauty professionally.

 ### AQUARIUS

To have Aquarius in your 10th House means you're building a legacy of innovation. You want to be known for being a changemaker, a rebel, the person who took a broken system and revolutionized it into something functional in the present and ready for the future. Aquarius's big-picture perspective often leads to a humanitarian or global approach to your career. You understand how everything is interconnected and are interested in creating meaningful and broad-ranging change. What is the community you are serving through your career? If not humanity broadly, then perhaps it's your local community, your labor union, your colleagues, or your students.

All Aquarius 10th House folks have Taurus as their Rising sign. That means you are motivated by Taurean energy (see chapter 3). Taurus Rising motivation blended with your innovative Aquarian career can have you interested in bringing your radical change into practical, tangible expression. You may also find that your Aquarian career is trying to revolutionize something Taurean in nature: tangible craftwork, art, agriculture, the environment, or financial systems. How does your Taurean motivation support the work of your Aquarian career? How does your core nature (Sun sign) factor in?

10

Houses
of Substance

Water

CANCER · SCORPIO · PISCES

▽

WATER AS THE ELEMENT of your Houses of Substance means that you approach finances and work from an emotional, relational, intuitive lens. When thinking about the skills with which you make money, your emotional intelligence, empathy, and interpersonal skills are what prove most satisfying as well as most effective. That isn't to say you don't possess many other skills that you use at work. You may have several placements in air signs, for example, and feel an affinity to cerebral work and problem-solving. Yet, when you consider your work life, what brings about your greatest professional successes? Is it your ability to form meaningful connections with colleagues or clients? Is it your intuitive understanding of the needs of others and ability to read the room? How does your relational acumen aid you in the workplace?

This description will likely ring true for you if you have several planets or luminaries in water signs. The more planetary and luminary placements in water signs you have, the more emotional and relational your nature will be. However, if you do not have many planets or luminaries placed in your Houses of Substance, you may not immediately recognize the role that your water qualities play in your work life. I once gave a reading to a medical professional who is a Sagittarius Sun, Gemini Rising, and Cancer Moon. The majority of his other planets are in fire and air signs, which might indicate that his life's purpose is about action, freedom, and intellectual pursuits. Yet, when it comes to work, because his Houses of Substance are all in water signs, his most important skills are his compassion and ability to form meaningful relationships with his patients. He identified that these relationships with patients are also the most satisfying aspect of his work. The water signature of his Houses of Substance speaks to the prominence of emotional intimacy in his career, even though he might not have consciously identified that as the through line. When reading the descriptions for your Houses of Substance, reflect on how the qualities of each sign show up in your work life and how they contribute to your professional success and satisfaction. The qualities of water may not be the most prominent in how you conceptualize your personality, and yet they are critical to your work life.

How can you align with the watery nature of your Houses of Substance, especially if you don't have many planets in water signs and feel disconnected from these approaches? Read through the description of your 2nd, 6th, and 10th House signs. See how they resonate with you. What about these descriptions feels invigorating and what seems draining? After reading the descriptions for your signs, answer the questions in **Cracking the Code: Your Work** to reflect on how past work experiences have capitalized on your watery work nature and how you can better align with your nature in the future.

HOUSES OF SUBSTANCE: WATER

Your 2nd House

The 2nd House pertains to your money and assets, how you manage them, as well as the skills with which you make them. Having a water sign in your 2nd House means that you approach making and managing your money through a relational, intuitive lens. Your emotional intelligence, empathy, and people skills are at the heart of how you make money, regardless of what line of work you're in. Let's take a closer look at your specific 2nd House sign.

CANCER

Cancer is noted for its ability to create home and family. When this ability is employed as a skill in the workplace, you make people feel included and at home, creating a sense of family with your colleagues, clients, or patrons. You have an innate ability to put others at ease. You're adept at anticipating the needs of others and making them feel cared for. These qualities can be used in any role from entry-level to CEO. Being able to connect with others so that they feel seen, included, and looked after encourages a happy work environment and fidelity from your employees and patrons. People want to be part of your work family.

The water signs are known for their receptivity, which is to say that they are receptive to the subtle cues from others. Whether picking up on other people's body language or their general vibe, water signs pick up on the emotional ripples others send out. But being receptive does not mean passive. Cancer is the cardinal water sign, which speaks to your ability to initiate and lead. Cancer, with its hard shell, can be stalwart in the face of difficulty, helping to keep the family together and hold down the fort. There is great strength and resilience in this sign. How does that show up for you in the workplace? How do you serve as the head of your work family? How do you bring people together and help them feel cared for? How do these Cancerian qualities serve as your professional superpowers?

SCORPIO

In terms of work, Scorpio brings an arsenal of useful skills. You are unflappable in the face of difficult conversations and situations, making you formidable in any workplace for your resilience but also enabling you to hold jobs that require you to deal with difficult, perhaps taboo topics. Scorpio in the 2nd House is a common setup for therapists, whose work centers on holding space for others as they process intense emotions, painful realities, and trauma. Scorpio is the sign of death, transformation, and rebirth, imbuing you with the unique ability to facilitate transformation for others. What underworld journeys do you guide? Whose hand do you hold through their darkest moments?

When the rest of society tries to look away and ignore the harsh realities of existence, Scorpio forces us all to face the truth. With Scorpio in the 2nd House, you possess the ability to uncover hidden things. You could use this skill as an auditor uncovering problematic corporate practices. You could be an author exposing truths about human nature. You could be an investigative journalist. There is an intensity and tenacity about you that, when focused on your work in this Scorpionic manner, will result in impressive professional results.

PISCES
In terms of work skills, Pisces can bring a systems-level view to whatever projects you work on. You see the big picture and how all aspects interconnect, where others might only see divisions and disjointed elements. You have an artist's imagination when it comes to work and can devise unique solutions to complex problems. All 2nd House Pisces folks have Aquarius as their Rising sign, and your Piscean prowess supports your Aquarian motivation to innovate and improve. Allowing yourself the space to daydream and think outside the box will be your key money-making strategy that will also make your work satisfying.

Pisces is the sign associated with universal love and compassion, which can be brought into the professional sphere in a number of ways. You may seek innovative solutions to humanitarian problems, perhaps through activism or technological innovation. On a more personal, localized level, Pisces in the 2nd House could speak to an acumen with understanding the emotional needs of others—a useful skill in collaboration, management, or working with patients and clients. Pisces is also known for its intuitive prowess, and you may have an uncanny knack for perceiving the nature of a problem and its solutions faster than others. Your intuitive powers may be employed to read people's emotions and needs so you can best serve them. How do systems thinking, intuition, and compassion show up in your career and work aspirations?

Your 6th House

The 6th House pertains to your day-to-day work, daily schedules, and regular habits. Having a water sign in your 6th House speaks to the relational, intuitive, and emotionally rich way in which you live out your day-to-day life. Because it deals with daily personal habits, this house also correlates to your physical health and the routine activities that foster it. Each water sign imparts its unique signature on the topics of this house. Let's take a closer look at your specific 6th House sign.

CANCER
Cancer in the 6th House speaks to a day-to-day work routine that involves caregiving and relationships. This signature is useful for people in management, because Cancer is a sign adept at bringing people together, organizing them, and evoking a sense of commitment and familial duty from staff. In a leadership position, you have the ability to create a tight-knit community, but even if you're not in that type of role, you work best in a team built on trust, mutual respect, and where each member feels responsible to one another. Overly isolating or competitive environments will be abrasive and taxing for you.

In terms of your personal health habits, family and home are what soothe and nourish you mentally and physically. Daily connection with family, however you define it, and relaxing in your private home space are your most critical daily practices.

SCORPIO

Scorpio is the Mars-ruled water sign. Mars is associated with sharp things: honed swords, cutting words, rapier wit. With Scorpio, Martian sharpness could be likened to a relentless drill boring a hole to get to the heart of things. Having Scorpio as your 6th House sign brings this focused willpower to your daily activities and work. You may find that you get lost in your work, perhaps even to the point of obsession. Finding work that is worthy of your Martian passion and Scorpionic emotional intensity will be most successful for you and most fulfilling. You aren't afraid of getting your hands dirty. You don't need work that is easy, you need work that matters.

In terms of personal health habits and your daily personal routines, mental health may be the greatest priority. With water for your Houses of Substance, it is likely that your work life is emotionally demanding and draining. How do you establish healthy boundaries from your work to protect your emotional well-being? How do you attend to your mental health regularly? Regular care of your mind and body will help avoid burnout and enable you to continue doing the work you're most passionate about.

PISCES

Pisces is the sign of dreams and imagination. It is the sign of self-dissolution, where you let go of the constraints of material reality and seek to connect with some higher truth. For you, your daily work isn't about rigid schedules or task lists or key performance indicators. You're striving to connect with the muse and channel eternal, ineffable wisdom (no pressure).

Whatever work you do, your daily routine must allow for imagination, daydreaming, and inspiration. Unless you have several planets in earth signs, you will likely struggle to adhere to strict timelines. This isn't a personal failing. It's just that rigidity is incompatible with how you get into flow with your work. And you must get into flow for your creativity and brilliance to arise. Structure will stifle this. More than just facilitating your work, prioritizing rest and daydreaming is essential to your mental and physical health. The more you can automate the mundane functions of life and work, the better.

Perhaps how your Pisces 6th House manifests is that your best daily work is motivated by compassion. All Pisces 6th House folks have Libra as their Rising sign, which means that you are motivated by a desire for peace, justice, and harmony. Pisces in the 6th House encourages you to let love and compassion structure your daily work to be most impactful and personally fulfilling.

Your 10th House

Whereas your 2nd House talks about work skills and the 6th House describes your daily work, the 10th House sign describes the nature of your overall career and public life. What is the legacy you're building? How are you cultivating the work and image you present to the world? Having a water sign in your 10th House speaks to the cultivation of a legacy evidencing your emotional intelligence and the meaningful relationships you've forged. Regardless of your profession, it will be how you've influenced and connected with people that you'll be most known for. Each water sign has a unique style. Let's take a closer look at your specific 10th House sign.

CANCER

With Cancer in your 10th House, your career is about nurturing and caregiving. Your legacy is building a sense of familial connection and devotion within your community. In the 10th House, this family could be your employees, your patrons, or perhaps the whole world. How is your work taking care of others? How are you building a sense of mutual obligation and love among the constituents of your community that helps them take care of each other? Your legacy is in the building of a home, and being in the 10th House places that home on the public stage.

All Cancer 10th House folks have Libra as their Rising sign, which is to say that you are motivated by a drive for balance, peace, and justice. You are also driven by beauty and connection. With this chart setup, you could be a lawyer or advocate, caretaking your clients through the legal system. You could be someone who designs beautiful home furnishings, creating homey spaces motivated by your drive to beautify. You may be a writer, seeking to build a community of global compassion through your work. How does your inclination for balance, beauty, and equality mesh with your work's watery nature of compassion and caregiving?

SCORPIO

With Scorpio as your 10th House, your legacy is guiding transformation. Scorpio is a sign of death and transformation, facilitating the transition from one space to another. Whether you're caring for someone as they pass from this life as a hospice nurse, working as a counselor helping people process trauma, helping society process our collective anguish in art, or sunsetting an obsolete computer program to make way for the new iteration, your career is about transitioning from something that must end to make way for what is to come next.

All Scorpio 10th Houses have Aquarius as their Rising sign, which means you are motivated by a drive to evaluate systems, destroy what is obsolete, and innovate for the future. You may feel a drive to improve for the benefit of the collective, be that your company, your local community, or even humanity. That drive ultimately compels you with Scorpionic intensity to dig for truth and bring to light all the broken, decaying detritus that had been hidden so that it can be examined, fixed, or discarded and replaced. You may find that your excavations reveal treasures long forgotten that need to be revived. This chart setup is that of the revolutionary, the rebel, the innovator, the interrogator. What change do you want to facilitate? What will be your legacy of transformation?

PISCES

With Pisces in your 10th House, your legacy is about connection. It is about understanding the ways in which all things are interconnected and interdependent. An environmental scientist with a Pisces 10th House may seek to understand how all things within an ecosystem are interrelated. A monk with a Pisces 10th House may work to shed the illusion that we are separate and seek to experience the truth that we are all one.

Indeed, there is something of a scientist monk about you. All people with Pisces as their 10th House have Gemini as their Rising sign (see chapter 3). You are motivated in life by an insatiable curiosity that isn't limited to a singular domain. Your understanding that everything is connected propels you to blend your vast and varied knowledge in innovative and exciting ways. You love to be surprised. You love to be astonished. You live to bask in the awe of something larger than yourself, while realizing that you, too, are part of that magnificence. Where do we experience the sublime more than in science and in spirituality? What work you ultimately do will be influenced by your other placements (see **Calibration** on balancing your chart). The essential energy you're seeking to create in your career is one that feeds your curiosity and allows you to return again and again to a state of enchanted wonder.

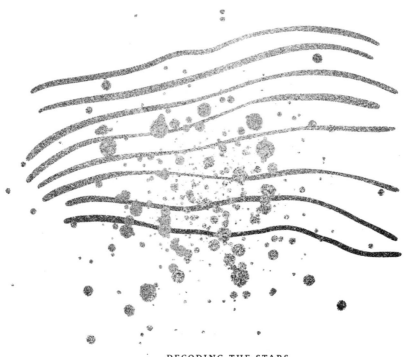

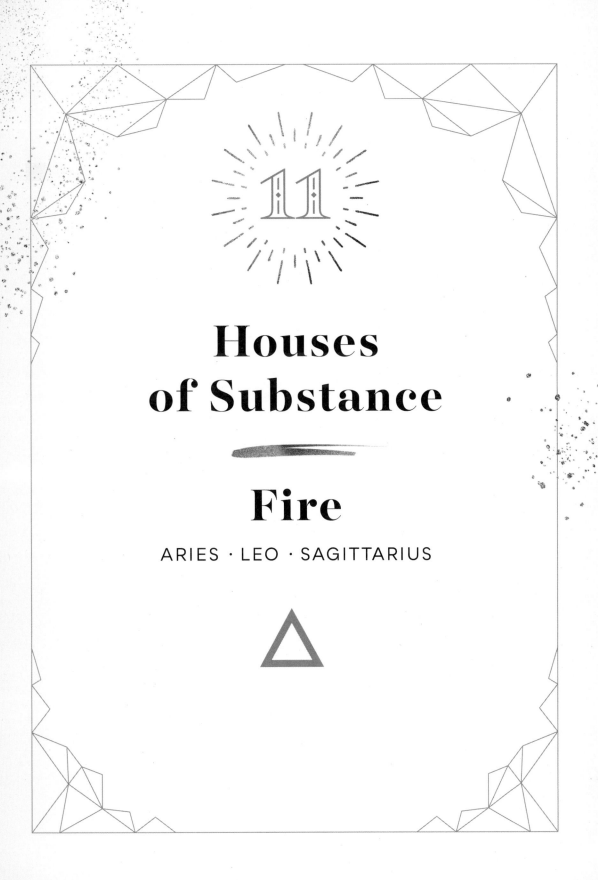

11

Houses of Substance

Fire

ARIES · LEO · SAGITTARIUS

△

FIRE AS THE ELEMENT of your Houses of Substance means that you approach finances and work in an action-oriented, passionate, adventurous, individualistic, and self-expressive way. When thinking about the skills with which you make money, your fiery, vibrant tenacity is what makes you most effective and satisfied at work. Each fire sign has its own unique qualities, so reading through your 2nd, 6th, and 10th House sign descriptions will help you to decipher the skills with which you make money, how you best engage with your daily work, and the ultimate goal of your career. This isn't to say that you don't have many other skills and gifts. If you have several planets placed in water signs, for example, you may have a marked acumen for building relationships that you utilize in your personal and professional life. When it comes to your work, though, it is the qualities of the fire signs that make you most successful and feel most in flow.

The descriptions in this chapter will likely ring true for you if you have several planets or luminaries in fire signs. The more planetary and luminary placements in fire signs you have, the more active and tenacious your character. However, if you do not have many planets or luminaries placed in your Houses of Substance, you may not immediately recognize the role that your fire qualities play in your work life. For example, I know a writer who is a Pisces Sun, Cancer Rising, Aries Moon, and her Houses of Substance are all fire signs. While she has a number of planets in fire signs, the majority of her placements are in water, and it took her some time to realize how fire shows up in her professional work. In particular, reflecting on her Leo 2nd House, she realized that shining her authentic light and her ability to perform (whether as a bartender or writer), have always been her most lucrative skills. Not having any planets in Leo, she hadn't given much attention to that aspect of her nature, and yet in looking at her work, it became clear how valuable her artistic self-expression is.

When reading the descriptions for your Houses of Substance, reflect on how the qualities of each sign show up in your work life and how they contribute to your professional success and satisfaction. The qualities of fire may not be the most prominent in how you conceptualize your personality, and yet they are critical to your work life.

How can you align with the fiery nature of your Houses of Substance, especially if you don't have many planets in fire signs and feel disconnected from these qualities? Read through the description of your 2nd, 6th, and 10th House signs. See how they resonate with you. What about these descriptions feels invigorating and what seems draining? After reading the descriptions for your signs, answer the questions in **Cracking the Code: Your Work** to reflect on how past work experiences have capitalized on your fiery work nature and how you can better align with your nature in the future.

Your 2nd House

The 2nd House pertains to your money and assets, how you manage them, as well as the skills with which you make them. Having a fire sign in your 2nd House means that you approach making and managing your money through tenacity and action. Each fire sign imbues its own style to this aspect of your life. Let's take a closer look at your specific 2nd House sign.

♈ ARIES

Aries is the cardinal fire sign and is compelled to initiate action. Your core money-making strategy is getting down to business. Not deliberating, revising, or collaborating, though you may be good at those things. What is most essential for you is the will and energy to get started. In the simplest sense, this could speak to your ability to begin new projects. Beyond that, you may have a drive to blaze new trails. Aries is a sign of independence and autonomy, so you may find that working for yourself and charting new professional paths is the most satisfying and successful for you.

Aries is also the archetypal warrior, so another professional skill you wield is your ability to fight. If you don't have many placements in fire signs, you may not immediately identify with this quality. But consider times in your professional life when you've had to go to the mat. How did you feel? How did that work out? In your work, do you serve as an advocate for yourself or others? Is this satisfying to you? Have you been successful in this role? All Aries 2nd House folks have Pisces as their Rising sign, so you are motivated by a sense of universal love and compassion. You care about others. How does this compassionate drive and warrior energy show up in your work?

♌ LEO

Leo is the sign of self-expression and performance. Ruled by the Sun, Leo calls you forth to shine your light into the world. This isn't a call to egoism. The Sun shines because it is its nature to shine. Likewise, Leo in the 2nd House calls you to shine your authentic self forth and the warmth of your self-expression will yield a bountiful harvest. Leo in the 2nd House doesn't mean you necessarily have to be an extrovert and put yourself on a physical stage to earn money. Instead, this placement indicates that you have some sort of artistic or performative flare that is compelling and lucrative for you. Whatever the stage and whoever the audience, your charisma and the way you craft the presentation of yourself and your story are entrancing.

The Leo qualities of your professional life may not be immediately apparent. But whenever you interact with others through any medium, you are presenting a version of yourself and crafting a story. You are looking to elicit a response, even if it is just to make your friend laugh. Think about the performative aspects of your work. When have you felt in flow when interacting with others? Consider times when you purposefully tried to be charismatic. How did that feel for you? How has that helped advance your career? What professional opportunities could you find to shine more of your Leo light?

SAGITTARIUS

Sagittarius is the sign of the adventurer and the sage. It is a sign that seeks wisdom through new experiences and through study. With Sagittarius as your 2nd House, your primary strategies for making money are your inquisitive nature, your adventurousness, and your vast knowledge and passion for learning. You may find yourself called to academia, but equally you may find that, in any role, your thirst for understanding and desire to teach come in handy. What role does learning, teaching, writing, or speaking play in your work?

As for adventure, Sagittarius is an intrepid sign. Your willingness to try new things and experience new places may prove to be key to your professional life, especially if you have planets in Sagittarius. You see opportunities at work, and that is a valuable skill. If your daily grind doesn't allow for much novelty, you will need to prioritize adventurous excursions in your personal life to support your physical well-being. If getting out to explore isn't something you can regularly do, you can scratch this itch through books and films that transport you to far off places or teach you new things.

Your 6th House

The 6th House pertains to your day-to-day work, daily schedules, and regular habits. Having a fire sign in your 6th House speaks to the action-oriented and passionate way in which you live out your day-to-day life. The 6th House also pertains to the daily rituals that foster our physical health, and the fire signs call you to an active lifestyle. Each fire sign imparts its unique signature on the topics of this house. Let's take a closer look at your specific 6th House sign.

ARIES

Aries is an independent, action-oriented sign. In your day-to-day work, there's nothing you abhor more than pointless meetings, bureaucracy, and navel-gazing. You don't want to admire a problem. You want to solve it. You want to be decisive. You are ready to cut to the chase. Finding job roles and work environments that let you get down to work and not hold you back are ideal. Truly, for all people with fire signs in their Houses of Substance, finding jobs that just allow you to start, work, and not jump endless meaningless hurdles is essential. Aries in particular desires autonomy. The more authority and independence you can get in your work, the better.

In terms of your personal health routines, Aries energy demands to be used up. It burns hot and fast. Left to simmer in your cubicle, your daily Aries energy might make you anxious. For your physical well-being, regular exercise, and perhaps particularly vigorous exercise, will help you maintain physical and mental well-being.

LEO

Leo is the sign of self-expression and performance. To have it in your 6th House of daily work and routines means you thrive with regular opportunities to shine. Speaking, performing, teaching, selling, persuading, acting—any activity that allows you to use your charisma and unique persona to captivate others. In what ways does your regular work prioritize stepping out on a stage (be that on a video chat with a client or a physical performance stage)? In those moments of performance, do you feel in flow? Do you receive positive feedback? How has putting yourself out there to perform benefited your career?

The 6th House is also the place of personal health and the daily habits that cultivate your health. With Leo here, there is a relationship between your sense of physical well-being and your ability to be seen and applauded. Fire signs in the 6th House require activity, novelty, and vibrancy to ensure your physical well-being. Meeting with friends, doing improv, or just engaging in meaningful self-expression at work will be nourishing to you.

SAGITTARIUS

Sagittarius is an inquisitive, optimistic sign that thrives on change and adventure. In your 6th House of daily routines, Sagittarius indicates that you work best when you have regular opportunities for new experiences. You need to feed your soul and your imagination in order to replenish your creative well. Adventures can be found on the hiking trail, on foreign shores, or in the library. The goal is to reenergize yourself and avoid ruts. If you are to continue shining the Leo light of your 2nd House, you're going to need revitalization and new ideas for your creative self-expression. Adventure makes you cultured, worldly, informed, and interesting.

Adventure, even just through your imagination, is what keeps you sane. The 6th House speaks to our physical health and the routines and habits that cultivate it. For you, engaging in intellectually and spiritually interesting activities, encountering new peoples and places, and generally expanding your horizons are key to maintaining your well-being.

HOUSES OF SUBSTANCE: FIRE

Your 10th House

Whereas your 2nd House talks about work skills and the 6th House describes your daily work, the 10th House sign describes the nature of your overall career and public life. What is the legacy you're building? How are you cultivating the work and image you present to the world? Having a fire sign in your 10th House speaks to the cultivation of a legacy evidencing your tenacity, passion, and adventurous spirit. Each fire sign has a unique style. Let's take a closer look at your specific 10th House sign.

ARIES

With Aries in the 10th House, your legacy is about blazing new trails. It is about your independence and your self-made success. Aries is not afraid to take up space and claim recognition for its excellence. With Leo in the 2nd House, your key professional skills for earning money are your authentic self-expression, so it makes sense that your career, then, is about you and the path that you forge for yourself. This could be as an entrepreneur or an artist, but equally it could indicate a general tenacity you bring to whatever career track you select. You could be the top sales rep for your company, using your Leonine charisma to close deals and climb the corporate ladder.

All Aries 10th House folks have Cancer as their Rising sign, which means you are motivated by a desire to cultivate family-like bonds, build a village, and nurture others. You may experience conflict between the individualism of an Aries drive in your career and this relationship-focused life motivation. Consider, though, the importance of community and relationships to your career. How do your Cancerian compassion and empathy enable you to connect better with others in your 2nd House Leo way? How do building community and caring for others blend with Aries energy as a warrior and advocate? How in your career have you already displayed evidence of your Cancerian caretaking, Leo performative skills, and Aries tenacity?

LEO

With Leo in the 10th House, your legacy is about self-expression and recognition. You have a contribution to make to the collective and you will be admired and honored for it. The tenacity of your fiery Houses of Substance spurs you on to accomplishments, and your Leo 10th House speaks to public recognition of your work. It is also a common signature for actors, musicians, and other celebrities in the public eye.

In what ways can you step into the limelight? Your audience doesn't have to be the world, but you are destined for some acclaim in whatever professional sphere you are in. Because Leo is ruled by the Sun, your Sun sign is particularly important to your career. Look to your Sun sign (chapter 1) and house (chapter 2) and consider how your core nature and preferred way of self-expression bring you recognition at work.

All Leo 10th House folks have Scorpio as their Rising sign, which means you are motivated by an intense desire to dig for the truth and emotional intensity in general. This may be why so many Scorpio Rising people become actors. In the acting profession, you can engage with the full spectrum of human experience and emotion. However, pushing towards any sort of revelation can scratch your Scorpionic itch, such as working as an auditor or investigator. How are you motivated to test the foundation, dig to find the bodies, or press for the truth? How does this fuel you to excel in your profession? How does it drive your self-expression and performance? When you think of the admiration and accolades you want conferred upon you professionally, what comes to mind? What do you want to be known for?

♐ SAGITTARIUS

With Sagittarius in the 10th House, your legacy is about adventure, learning, and seeking wisdom. Your career calls you to study, to teach, and to learn through varied experiences. From the vast wisdom you accumulate, you serve as a teacher and a sage. Sagittarius's drive to learn stems from a yearning to understand the great truths of our world. Who are we? Why are we here? This could lead your career down a spiritual, philosophical, or scientific path.

All Sagittarius 10th House folks have Pisces as their Rising sign, which means that you are motivated by a desire for connection. Pisces wants to break down boundaries, even to dissolve one's sense of self, to touch the ineffable and experience divine transcendence. This drive for spiritual epiphany supports your Sagittarian career of seeking and sharing wisdom. The ruler of Sagittarius is Jupiter, which is also the traditional ruling planet of Pisces. It is the planet of expansion, philosophy, and faith. There is a strong signature in your chart for seeking wisdom and sharing it.

But perhaps spirituality and faith feel too foreign to you. In another sense, Pisces Rising is motivated to understand the connections among all things. Perhaps your interest is in understanding emotional connections and how people interrelate. Perhaps you're interested in ecological interdependence. Perhaps you're interested in physics and discovering a viable unified theory. For any of these drives, a Sagittarian career of travel, study, and teaching would be successful and fulfilling. What connections are you driven by (review your Pisces Rising in chapter 3)? What knowledge do you want to seek and teach in your career? What discoveries or wisdom do you want to be known for?

HOUSES OF SUBSTANCE: FIRE

CRACKING THE CODE
YOUR WORK

YOUR CORE SELF, YOUR MOTIVATION, AND YOUR WORK

When thinking about what careers are in alignment with your true nature, you'll want to synthesize several elements of your chart together to get a clearer picture.

List keywords that resonate with you for the following:

What skills of your 2nd House sign do you use (or would like to use) to make money?

What qualities of your core nature (Sun sign) do you use (or would like to use) at work?

How does your work tap into your essential motivation in life (Rising sign)? How would you like it to?

INSIGHTS FROM WHERE YOU'VE BEEN

All of your past professional, volunteer, and hobby experiences are a treasure trove of information about what aligns with your nature and what doesn't. Even if it was a job you hated, there are likely parts of it that you enjoyed or that used your unique skills.

How did your previous jobs use your specialized skills (2nd House)?
How did you feel while using those skills?

Which day-to-day schedules and habits have worked well for you? Which haven't?
How does this correspond to the nature of your 6th House?

In what ways did your day-to-day work (6th House) support long-term work and career goals (10th House)? Did you find this daily work more fulfilling because it clearly tied to building your career?

In what ways have past jobs aligned with your 10th House sign?
Did those aspects feel satisfying and would you like to seek out more of that in your career?

In what ways have past jobs focused on qualities misaligned or antithetical to the style
of your 10th House sign? Can you avoid those qualities in future jobs?

YOUR LEGACY

Taking into consideration your core nature (Sun placement), your motivation
(Rising sign and ruler), your skills (2nd House), how you best work day-to-day (6th House),
and the overall style of your career (10th House), what career paths call to you? What excites you?
What do you want to be known for? What will be your legacy?

Calibration

WE'VE COVERED a lot of ground in this book so far. We've discussed your core nature, what energizes you, and how you shine by interpreting your Sun sign and house. We've unpacked what motivates you and where your life is being steered by digging into your Rising sign and its ruler. We took a deep dive into your Moon sign and house to identify what most helps you feel emotionally secure and balanced. We then considered your relationship to money, your work life, and your career through interpreting your Houses of Substance.

But what do you do with all that information? How do you put it all together to create a cohesive narrative about your life's purpose?

One of the main challenges with decoding your birth chart is knowing how to balance the different elements. Not all the elements of your chart are equally impactful in your life. Some placements you will feel more. Some elements will support each other, while others conflict. Decoding your birth chart requires **calibration**: assessing each element in relation to one another to get a clear picture of your life's purpose.

Weight

Your chart has all twelve zodiacal signs, twelve houses, and four elements, but which signs feel most expressed in your personality and life? Which house topics are most critical to you? To answer these questions, we must look to where the planets, luminaries, and major points (Ascendant and Midheaven) are placed in your chart. The more celestial objects you have in a given sign, house, or element, the more weight that sign, house, or element carries in your life. You will have houses and signs and maybe even elements that have no objects in them, and that is totally fine and completely normal. Your celestial cocktail is bespoke and beautiful. We all find challenges in our charts, but also strengths. Remember you are, above all, here to be you.

Looking at your birth chart, complete the following tables to get a sense of which signs, houses, and elements carry the most weight.

	CELESTIAL OBJECT	SIGN	HOUSE	ELEMENT
AC	Ascendant point		1st	
MC	Midheaven point			
☉	Sun			
☽	Moon			
☿	Mercury			
♀	Venus			
♂	Mars			
♃	Jupiter			
♄	Saturn			
♅	Uranus			

CELESTIAL OBJECT		SIGN	HOUSE	ELEMENT
♆	Neptune			
♇	Pluto			

HOUSE	NUMBER OF OBJECTS
1st	
2nd	
3rd	
4th	
5th	
6th	
7th	
8th	
9th	
10th	
11th	
12th	

SIGN		NUMBER OF OBJECTS
♈	Aries	
♉	Taurus	
♊	Gemini	
♋	Cancer	
♌	Leo	
♍	Virgo	
♎	Libra	
♏	Scorpio	
♐	Sagittarius	
♑	Capricorn	
♒	Aquarius	
♓	Pisces	

ELEMENT	NUMBER OF OBJECTS
Earth	
Air	
Water	
Fire	

225

Balancing Your Chart

Now that you've identified where the objects in your chart are placed, you can interpret what that means. What is your unique balance of elements, signs, and houses in your chart?

YOUR ELEMENTAL BALANCE

In which elements are your luminaries, planets, and points most concentrated? Do you have a pretty even balance, or do you have many objects in just one or two elements? What elements have few or no objects? Being weighted toward an element will give you certain proclivities, superpowers, and challenges. Whatever your elemental balance, I encourage you to embrace it and the gifts it brings into your life and the collective. As you read through the description of your main elements, ask yourself:

> ➤ How is my life's purpose colored by my elemental nature?

> ➤ How can I honor and lean into this aspect of myself more authentically in my life?

> ➤ When do I feel in flow using my elemental superpowers?

> ➤ How are my challenging aspects a blessing? How have I learned from these struggles?

> ➤ What external resources and skills can help fill my elemental gaps when I need support?

 EARTH

Superpowers: practical, methodical, persistent
Challenges: obstinance, being overly literal, being materialistic

If your objects are concentrated in earth signs, you're likely to be a grounded person. Your overall vibe will be still and calming, especially if your objects are concentrated in Taurus or Capricorn. Virgo's Mercurial energy can sometimes feel more like a buzz of activity and thought. You'll be particularly capable of seeing projects through and having tangible results for your work. You're not all talk. You may struggle with feeling inspired, being too focused on the real world and the tasks at hand to allow your imagination to wander. You may also get stuck—in your ways, in a job, in a relationship. Commitment can be a blessing and a curse.

AIR

Superpowers: communicative, inquisitive, cerebral
Challenges: stuck in your head, scattered, lack of follow-through

If your objects are concentrated in air signs, you're likely to be a chatty, thoughtful person. Smart, interested, and inquisitive, you like to learn and are a confident and capable communicator. Being airy can also feel ungrounded, like you're too in your head and unable to connect your mental gymnastics to the real world or tangible outcomes. Philosophy has its value, but you may also have projects you want to finish. You also might have so many interests or projects that you get overwhelmed. You may also struggle to attain mastery, which requires commitment and persistence. On the other hand, your cornucopia of interests and knowledge makes you uniquely able to draw connections across domains of knowledge and come up with ingenious solutions.

 WATER

Superpowers: emotionally intelligent, intuitive, relational
Challenges: emotional volatility, being other-focused, setting boundaries

If your objects are concentrated in water signs, you're likely to be a caring person interested in meaningful relationships and endeavors that help others. Highly empathetic, you're adept at sensing other people's emotions. You may also be generally intuitive in your knowing. You may at times find your emotions volatile and challenging. This isn't to say that being emotional is problematic, rather that feeling out of control is uncomfortable and taxing. Developing emotional regulation skills and self-awareness can help you engage with your emotions in healthier ways. You may also have a tendency to put others before yourself to your detriment. Finding a balance between self and other and establishing healthy boundaries will be particularly useful to you.

 FIRE

Superpowers: passionate, action-oriented, vivacious
Challenges: emotional volatility, unstructured, lack of follow-through

If your objects are concentrated in fire signs, you're likely to be a vibrant, fun, action-oriented individual. You're full of life and have ease kicking off new projects and adventures. You have a zest for life that is contagious. Like water signs, you may struggle with volatile emotions, feeling easily set off. Fire signs live in the moment and so emotions can feel all-encompassing in their immediacy. This isn't to say that experiencing and expressing emotions is problematic, rather that feeling overwhelmed and subject to your emotions can be challenging and exhausting. Similar to water signs (who struggle with emotional volatility but for different reasons), developing emotional regulation skills and self-awareness will be crucial for you. This can help you feel more steady and less beholden to extreme emotions. Like air signs, you may also struggle with follow-through, being so exuberant to follow the inspiration of the moment. You may also find you get bored before a project comes to completion. Finding external accountability and structures to help you see things through can aid you in achieving your goals.

YOUR SIGN AND HOUSE BALANCE

How are the planets, luminaries, and points dispersed in your chart by sign and house? Are they distributed among many signs and houses, or concentrated in a few? As with the elements, a concentration of objects in a single sign means you will identify more with the qualities of that sign than others. That sign's nature will be more prominent in your personality. If you have planets concentrated in a single sign, then you will also have them concentrated in the house that sign occupies, drawing focus to the areas of life indicated by that house (see page 17 for a quick guide to the house meanings).

The balance of celestial objects in the signs helps you develop a more nuanced understanding of your nature. One pitfall people can experience is overidentifying with their Sun sign, when they are actually much more complex. Conversely, someone might feel like they don't connect with their Sun sign, but that's because they have several planets concentrated in a different sign, influencing their personality and how they experience the world.

While the concentration of objects draws focus to that sign and amplifies its expression in your life, not all objects are weighted equally. It's important to note that the Sun, Rising, and Moon signs still carry the most weight, which is why we focused so heavily on them in this book.

The Story of a Birth Chart

So how does calibration work in practice? How do you balance the elements and develop a story about your life's purpose from your birth chart? Let's consider an example.

This individual is a water- and earth-heavy person. Their Sun and Rising signs are both water, which significantly imbues their personality with water qualities. Jupiter and Pluto also being in water signs further amplify the focus on emotional connection and intuition in this person's personality and life's purpose. This person is likely to be motivated to seek out emotionally rich and intense experiences (Scorpio Rising). Their core nature is deeply interested in the connection between all things and perhaps seeks opportunities for the dissolution of self to experience some greater truth or connection (Pisces Sun). Pisces Sun folks often find this connection to a higher ideal or spiritual oneness through art; with this person's Sun in the 5th House of creativity, we could expect such a person to be drawn to artistic expression motivated by their drive to interrogate the depth of human emotion, especially taboo topics (Scorpio Rising).

EXAMPLE CHART

BIRTH DATE: February 26, 1990
BIRTH TIME: 11:27 p.m.
BIRTH LOCATION: Los Angeles, California

ELEMENT	NUMBER OF OBJECTS
Earth	5
Air	1
Water	4
Fire	2

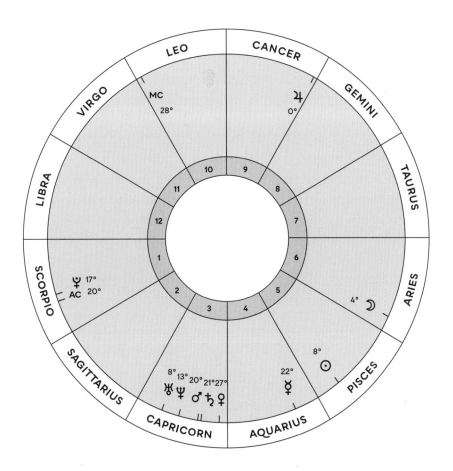

While a water-heavy person might struggle with structure and stamina, this person has five planets in Capricorn (Venus, Mars, Saturn, Uranus, and Neptune). Indeed, they have more objects in earth than water. Because two of their big three objects (their Sun and Rising) are in water, it's likely they still feel a prominent watery nature. They will, however, also have a sense of earthy stability and especially Capricorn qualities, like being achievement oriented, having the ability to accomplish tasks, and wanting to build a legacy. The watery nature of their Pisces core essence might get lost in imagination and inward reflection. However, the concentration in Capricorn should indicate a strong level of drive to accomplish tasks and projects, counteracting some of the more challenging aspects of water.

A great deal of focus is being pulled to the 3rd House, which contains Capricorn and five planets. Notably, the Rising sign ruler is placed here, steering the individual's life toward 3rd House topics. Communication is likely to be a key element of their life's purpose. Taken together, the Sun in the 5th House of creativity, a concentration of planets in the house of communication, and the Midheaven in Leo in the 10th House of career and public life, it seems likely that the individual would be pulled toward artistic expression in the public sphere. Leo in the 10th House could indicate that the career is about performance or exhibiting work publicly, and the concentration of planets in the house of communication means they have a message to share and the ability to share it. The lack of air placements in this person's chart might indicate that their message is communicated through nonlinguistic means (e.g., music or visual art). However, having so many planets in the house of communication generally speaks to acumen with all forms of communication and especially writing and speaking. They might be focused on creating an emotional experience for their audience (the water focus of the Sun and Rising).

Their fire Moon in Aries will likely give them tenacity in expressing their emotions and advocating for themselves. That the Moon is in the 6th House of day-to-day work and the Midheaven is in the 10th House draws focus on the person expressing their life's purpose through their work and career. That the person's Moon is placed in the 6th House of day-to-day work indicates that they will find emotional well-being through an active (Aries) approach to their work life, further supporting the Capricorn focus on achievement, likely through their profession.

This is certainly not the only way to interpret this chart, but I hope that this example illustrates some of the thinking that goes into interpreting a person's birth chart and developing a narrative about their life's purpose.

DECODING THE STARS

The Story of You

The more you reflect on your astrology, the more you'll identify what resonates and you'll develop a story of yourself and your life's purpose that is meaningful to you. The previous example hopefully helps get you started, but if you're feeling stuck, consider the following approach:

➢ Start with your Sun sign to understand your core nature and where and how you want to shine that nature (Sun house).

➢ Consider your Rising sign to understand what motivates you and consider how that motivation supports and blends with your core nature.

➢ Consider your Moon sign and how the values and qualities of that sign support or conflict with the nature of your Sun and Rising signs. Reflect on your Moon house, where you find emotional security and well-being, and how that relates to your Sun house and Rising sign ruler's house topics in terms of your life's purpose.

➢ Look to see if you have any signs with concentrations of three or more objects. Consider how the nature of that sign and the topics of that house give information about prominent qualities of your nature and prominent topics in your life.

➢ Think about the balance of elements in your chart, what superpowers that gifts you with, and also the challenges that might indicate.

This should give you a solid start to decoding your birth chart and understanding your life's purpose. Know that as you grow and change, the expression of each placement will mature, too. An immature Aries Moon may be quick to feel slighted, always seeking out righteous retribution, whereas a mature Aries Moon will know when to choose their battles. Though the birth chart is static, your expression of it is ever evolving. This evolution is what makes studying your astrology worthwhile: through self-reflection, you will not just own your true nature but also cultivate the best expression of it.

Ultimately, decoding your birth chart is a means of self-reflection to help you write the story of yourself. Through this practice, you can become the author of your story, rather than a passive reader of what has unconsciously unfolded. While astrology is predicated on the belief that you were fated to be you, it also provides the tools for you to make the best out of your beautiful, unique self. The birth chart speaks to your nature and your potential. You have the power to harness the wisdom hidden in your stars to build a life of purpose, meaning, and joy.

About the Author

ALLISON SCOTT is a book editor, astrologer, and creativity midwife based in Southern California. Through horoscopes, individual astrology readings, and coaching, she helps people understand and connect with their life's purpose and innate creativity, helping artists bring their creative work into being. You can connect with Allison on Instagram @conjuringthemuse and find out more about working with her at conjuringthemuse.com.

Acknowledgments

This book wouldn't be possible without the scholarship of the astrological community. My practice has been especially influenced by astrologers who've worked tirelessly to rediscover and revive Hellenistic astrology, particularly Demetra George, Chris Brennan, and Chani Nicholas. To these astrologers, to their teachers and colleagues, and to the whole lineage of astrologers, I express my gratitude.

It is not an overstatement to say that I am the astrologer I am today because of the kindness and encouragement of Colin Bedell. You are a bright light in the world. Shine on, friend.

To the team at Quarto, I am so grateful for this opportunity and for the beautiful book we've created together. Thanks to Rage Kindelsperger for seeing something worthwhile in my ramblings. Thanks to my editors Katie Moore and Elizabeth You for their guidance and support. To Elizabeth, especially, I am so grateful. This book would not exist without your insightful feedback, warm encouragement, and exceptional professionalism. You are a gifted editor, and I am so lucky to have worked with you on my first book.

To my friend and agent, Marleen Seegers, words can't express how grateful I am to have you in my life. You are wonderful and brilliant, and I am so thankful that fate brought us together.

I am infinitely grateful to my community of friends and family, whose love and support create a safe harbor from which I'm able to take risks and strive for my dreams. Special thanks to Sarah, Natalee, Cathleen, Ceryn, Sassy, Justine, Jessie, Katrina, Jamie, Mark, Andrew, and Paul. I am a better person for having you all in my life. This book exists because of you. Thank you.

233

References

Barnes, Jason. 2011. "Is a Moon Necessary for a Planet to Support Life?" Interview by Ira Flatow. *Science Friday*, NPR, November 18, 2011. Audio, 12:23. https://www.npr.org/2011/11/18/142512088/is-a-moon-necessary-for-a-planet-to-support-life.

Brennan, Chris. 2017. *Hellenistic Astrology: The Study of Fate and Fortune*. Denver, CO: Amor Fati.

Buis, Alan. 2020. "Milankovitch (Orbital) Cycles and Their Role in Earth's Climate." NASA Global Climate Change, February 27, 2020. https://climate.nasa.gov/news/2948/milankovitch-orbital-cycles-and-their-role-in-earths-climate.

Csikszentmihalyi, Mihaly. 2013. *Creativity: The Psychology of Discovery and Invention*. New York: Harper Perennial.

Gaskell, Elizabeth. 1857. *The Life of Charlotte Brontë*. Volume 1. London: Smith, Elder, and Co.

George, Demetra. 2008. *Astrology and the Authentic Self: Integrating Traditional and Modern Astrology to Uncover the Essence of the Birth Chart*. Lake Worth, FL: Ibis Press.

hooks, bell. 1994. "bell hooks by Lawrence Chua." Interview by Lawrence Chua. *BOMB Magazine*, July 1, 1994. https://bombmagazine.org/articles/bell-hooks.

Hsu, Hua. 2021. "The Revolutionary Writing of bell hooks." *The New Yorker*, December 15, 2021. https://www.newyorker.com/culture/postscript/the-revolutionary-writing-of-bell-hooks.

Kane, Stephen R. 2017. "Worlds without Moons: Exomoon Constraints for Compact Planetary Systems." *Astrophysical Journal Letters* 839, no. 2 (April). https://doi.org/10.3847/2041-8213/aa6bf2.

Margesson, Maud. 1928. *The Brontës and Their Stars*. London: Rider and Co.

Nicholas, Chani. 2020. *You Were Born for This*. New York: HarperOne.

Renstrom, Christopher. 2020. *The Cosmic Calendar: Using Astrology to Get in Sync with Your Best Life*. New York: TarcherPerigee.

Vireck, George Sylvester. 1929. "What Life Means to Einstein: An Interview with George Sylvester Vireck." *Saturday Evening Post*, October 26, 1929. https://www.saturdayeveningpost.com/wp-content/uploads/satevepost/what_life_means_to _einstein.pdf

REFERENCES

Index

1st House
    Air element and, 168
    balance calibration, 228
    Earth element and, 168
    Fire element and, 168
    meaning, 55
    Moon and, 166, 168
    Rising sign, 14, 52, 53, 118
    Sun and, 56–57
    Uranus in, 198
2nd House
    Air element and, 201–202
    balance calibration, 228
    Earth element and, 194–195
    Fire element and, 215–216
    as House of Substance, 186, 188,
        190, 191
    meaning, 55
    Moon and, 166, 169
    Rising sign, 119
    Sun and, 58–59
    Water element and, 208–209
3rd House
    balance calibration, 228
    communication style, 61
    Jupiter in, 107
    meaning, 55
    Moon and, 166, 170
    Rising sign, 120, 230
    Sun and, 60–61
4th House
    balance calibration, 228
    meaning, 55
    Moon and, 148, 166, 171
    Rising sign, 121
    Sun and, 62–63
    work-life balance, 74–75
5th House
    Air element and, 172
    balance calibration, 228

creative style, 65
    Earth element and, 172
    Fire element and, 172
    meaning, 55
    Moon and, 165, 166, 172
    Rising sign, 122, 131
    Sun and, 64–65, 228, 230
6th House
    Air element and, 202–203
    balance calibration, 228
    Earth element and, 195–197
    Fire element and, 216–217
    as House of Substance, 187, 188,
        190, 191
    meaning, 55
    Moon and, 166, 173, 230
    Rising sign, 123
    Sun and, 66–67
    Water element and, 209–210
7th House
    balance calibration, 228
    meaning, 55
    Moon and, 166, 174
    Rising sign, 124
    Sun and, 68–69, 118
8th House
    balance calibration, 228
    meaning, 55
    Moon and, 166, 175
    Rising sign, 125
    Sun and, 70–71
9th House
    balance calibration, 228
    inquiry approach, 73
    Jupiter in, 107
    meaning, 55
    Medium Coeli (MC) in, 190
    Moon and, 166, 176, 181
    Rising sign, 126
    Sun and, 72–73, 81

10th House
    Air element and, 204–205
    balance calibration, 228
    Earth element and, 197–198
    Fire element and, 218–219
    as House of Substance, 187, 188,
        190, 191
    meaning, 55
    Medium Coeli (MC) in, 230
    Moon and, 148, 166, 177
    Rising sign, 127
    Sun and, 62, 74–75, 181
    Uranus in, 198
    Water element and, 211–212
    work-life balance, 74–75
11th House
    Air element and, 178
    balance calibration, 228
    Earth element and, 178
    Fire element and, 178
    meaning, 55
    Moon and, 148, 166, 178
    Rising sign, 128
    Sun and, 76–77
12th House
    balance calibration, 228
    meaning, 55
    Moon and, 166, 179
    Rising sign, 129
    Sun and, 78–79

A
Air element
    1st House and, 168
    2nd House and, 201–202
    5th House and, 172
    6th House and, 202–203
    10th House and, 204–205
    11th House and, 178
    Aquarius and, 18, 48–49, 160

balance calibration, 227
description of, 25
Gemini and, 18, 32–33, 94, 201,
    202, 204
Houses of Substance and, 187,
    188, 200–205
inquiry approach, 73
Libra and, 18, 40–41, 102, 201,
    203, 204
Rising sign, 87, 94, 102
Sun and, 25, 32–33
Aquarius
    2nd House and, 202
    6th House and, 203
    10th House and, 205
    balance calibration, 228
    communication style, 61
    community style, 77
    creative style, 65
    Fixed modality, 18, 48–49
    Moon and, 160–161
    Rising sign, 89, 110–111, 209, 211
    Saturn and, 18, 48–49, 110–111,
        115, 116
    Uranus and, 18, 48–49, 116, 160,
        202
    Sun and, 48–49
    symbol, 18
Aries
    2nd House and, 215
    6th House and, 216
    10th House and, 218
    balance calibration, 228
    Cardinal modality, 18, 28–29,
        90, 215
    communication style, 61
    community style, 77
    creative style, 65
    Mars and, 28–29, 90–91, 115
    Moon and, 140–141, 231
    Rising sign, 90–91, 198
    ruling planets, 18, 28–29, 115
    Sun and, 28–29
    symbol, 18
Ascendant point
    birth chart and, 14, 19
    definition of, 16
    determining, 14, 15, 16

Rising sign and, 53
zodiacal sign and, 14

B
birth charts
    Albert Einstein, 80–81
    bell hooks, 130–131
    calibration example, 228–230
    ecliptic, 13
    Emily Brontë, 180–181
    glyphs, 13
    introduction to, 13
    luminaries, 19
    My Astro Code summary, 21
    parts diagram, 13
    pulling, 20
    resources for, 20
    Rising sign and, 14–15
    Ursula K. Le Guin, 14, 15, 16, 17

C
calibration
    approach to, 231
    birth chart example, 228–230
    elemental balance, 226–228
    house balance, 228
    introduction to, 223
    Rising sign and, 231
    sign balance, 228
    weight, 224–225
Cancer
    2nd House and, 208
    6th House and, 209–210
    10th House and, 211
    balance calibration, 228
    Cardinal modality, 18, 34–35,
        208
    communication style, 61
    community style, 77
    creative style, 65
    Moon and, 18, 34–35, 96–97,
        115, 146–147, 181
    Rising sign, 96–97, 218
    Sun and, 34–35, 58
    symbol, 18
Capricorn
    2nd House and, 195–196
    6th House and, 196–197

10th House and, 198
balance calibration, 228
Cardinal modality, 18, 46–47,
    108, 204
communication style, 61
community style, 77
creative style, 65
Moon and, 158–159
Rising sign, 108–109, 204–205
Saturn and, 18, 46–47, 108–109,
    115
Sun and, 46–47
symbol, 18
Uranus and, 158
Cardinal modality
    Aries, 18, 28–29, 90, 215
    Cancer, 18, 34–35, 208
    Capricorn, 18, 46–47, 108, 204
    description of, 25
    Libra, 18, 40–41, 102, 204
    Rising sign, 88

E
Earth element
    1st House and, 168
    2nd House and, 194–195
    5th House and, 172
    6th House and, 195–197
    10th House and, 197–198
    11th House and, 178
    balance calibration, 226
    Capricorn, 18, 46–47, 195,
        196–197, 198, 226
    description of, 25
    Houses of Substance and, 187,
        188, 193–198
    inquiry approach, 73
    Rising sign, 87
    Sun and, 25
    Taurus, 18, 30–31, 92, 93, 194,
        195–196, 197
    Virgo, 18, 38–39, 150, 194–195,
        196, 198, 226
ecliptic
    birth chart and, 13
    Medium Coeli (MC) and, 19, 190
    Rising sign and, 15
elements. *See individual elements*

essential points. *See* Ascendant point; Medium Coeli (MC)

F

Fire element
    1st House and, 168
    2nd House and, 215–216
    5th House and, 172
    6th House and, 216–217
    10th House and, 218–219
    11th House and, 178
    Aries, 18, 28–29, 90, 140, 215, 216, 218, 230
    balance calibration, 227–228
    description of, 25
    Houses of Substance and, 187, 188, 214–219
    inquiry approach, 73
    Leo, 18, 36–37, 215, 217, 218–219
    Rising sign, 87, 190
    Sagittarius, 18, 44–45, 107, 216, 217, 219
    Sun and, 25, 28–29, 73
Fixed modality
    Aquarius, 18, 48–49
    description of, 25
    Leo, 18, 36–37
    Rising sign, 88
    Scorpio, 18, 42–43, 105
    Sun and, 25
    Taurus, 18, 30–31, 92, 93, 194

G

Gemini
    2nd House and, 201
    6th House and, 202
    10th House and, 204
    balance calibration, 228
    communication style, 61
    community style, 77
    creative style, 65
    Sun and, 32–33
    Mercury and, 18, 32–33, 94–95, 115, 144, 201, 204
    Moon and, 144–145
    Mutable modality, 18, 32–33, 59, 94, 145, 201, 204
    Rising sign, 94–95

Sun and, 32–33
symbol, 18

H

Hellenistic astrology, 14, 86
Houses of Substance. *See also individual houses*
    Air element and, 187, 188, 200–205
    birth chart and, 188–190
    Earth element and, 187, 188, 193–198
    Fire element and, 187, 188, 214–219
    Medium Coeli (MC) and, 190
    Rising sign and, 190
    Water element and, 187, 188, 207–212

J

Jupiter
    3rd House and, 107
    9th House and, 107
    Pisces and, 18, 50–51, 112–113, 115
    Sagittarius and, 18, 44–45, 106–107, 115, 156, 219
    speed, 116
    symbol, 19
    transit speed, 116

L

Leo
    2nd House and, 215
    6th House and, 217
    10th House and, 197, 218–219, 230
    balance calibration, 228
    communication style, 61
    community style, 77
    creative style, 65
    Fixed modality, 18, 36–37
    Moon and, 148–149, 177
    Rising sign, 98–99, 197
    Sun and, 18, 36–37, 56, 98–99, 115
    symbol, 18
Libra
    2nd House and, 201–202
    6th House and, 16, 203, 210

10th House and, 204–205, 210
balance calibration, 228
Cancer and, 211
Cardinal modality, 18, 40–41, 102, 204
communication style, 61
community style, 77
creative style, 65
Moon and, 152–153
Pisces and, 210
Rising sign, 102–103, 210, 211
Sun and, 40–41, 60
symbol, 18
Venus and, 18, 40–41, 102–103, 115, 152, 153, 201, 203, 205
luminaries. *See* Moon; Sun

M

Mars
    Aries and, 28–29, 90–91, 115
    Scorpio and, 42–43, 104–105, 115, 154, 210
    speed, 116
    symbol, 19
    transit speed, 116
Medium Coeli (MC)
    9th House and, 190
    10th House and, 230
    definition of, 13, 19
    Houses of Substance and, 190
Mercury
    Gemini and, 18, 32–33, 94–95, 115, 144, 201, 204
    speed, 116
    symbol, 19
    transit speed, 116
    Virgo and, 38–39, 100–101, 115, 118, 144, 150, 194
Midheaven. *See* Medium Coeli (MC)
modality. *See* Cardinal modality; Fixed modality; Mutable modality
Moon
    1st House and, 166, 168
    2nd House and, 166, 169
    3rd House and, 166, 170
    4th House and, 148, 166, 171
    5th House and, 165, 166, 172

6th House and, 166, 173, 230
7th House and, 166, 174
8th House and, 166, 175
9th House and, 166, 176, 181
10th House and, 148, 166, 177
11th House and, 148, 166, 178
12th House and, 166, 179
Aquarius and, 160–161
Aries and, 140–141
calibration and, 231
Cancer and, 18, 34–35, 96–97, 115, 146–147, 181
Capricorn and, 158–159
Gemini and, 144
Leo and, 148–149, 177
Libra and, 152–153
Pisces and, 162–163
placement of, 54, 116
purpose and, 139
Sagittarius and, 156–157
Scorpio and, 154–155
sign introduction, 136–137
symbol, 19
Taurus and, 142
Virgo and, 150–151
Mutable modality
    description of, 25
    Gemini, 18, 32–33, 59, 94, 145, 201, 204
    Pisces, 18, 50–51, 59
    Rising sign, 88
    Sagittarius, 18, 44–45, 59, 106
    Virgo, 18, 38–39, 59, 100
My Astro Code summary, 21

N
Neptune
    Pisces and, 18, 50–51, 116
    speed, 116
    symbol, 19
    transit speed, 116

P
Pisces
    2nd House and, 209
    3rd House and, 60
    6th House and, 66, 210
    9th House and, 81

10th House and, 212, 219
12th House and, 78
balance calibration, 228
communication style, 61
community style, 77
creative style, 65
Jupiter and, 18, 50–51, 112–113, 115
Libra and, 210
Moon and, 162–163
Mutable modality, 18, 50–51, 59
Neptune and, 18, 50–51, 116
Rising sign, 112–113
Sun and, 50–51, 60
symbol, 18
planets. *See individual planets*
Pluto
    Scorpio and, 18, 42–43, 116, 154–155
    speed, 116
    symbol, 19
    transit speed, 116

R
Rising sign
    1st House, 14, 52, 53, 118
    2nd House, 119
    3rd House, 120, 230
    4th House, 121
    5th House, 122, 131
    6th House, 123
    7th House, 124
    8th House, 125
    9th House, 126
    10th House, 127
    11th House, 128
    12th House, 129
    Air element and, 87, 94, 102
    Aquarius, 89, 110–111, 209, 211
    Aries, 90–91, 198
    birth chart and, 14–15
    calibration and, 231
    Cancer, 96–97, 218
    Capricorn, 108–109, 204–205
    Cardinal modality, 88
    Earth element and, 87
    ecliptic and, 15
    Fire element and, 87, 190

Fixed modality, 88
Gemini, 94–95, 212
houses and, 14–15, 133
Houses of Substance and, 190
Leo, 98–99, 197
Libra, 102–103, 210, 211
Mutable modality, 88
Pisces, 112–113, 219
placement of, 54, 116
rectification and, 15
ruling planets, 89
Sagittarius, 106–107, 198
Scorpio, 104–105, 219
Taurus, 92–93
traditional rulership, 115
Virgo, 100–101, 204
Water element and, 87
ruling planets. *See specific planets*

S
Sagittarius
    2nd House and, 216
    6th House and, 217
    10th House and, 198, 219
    balance calibration, 228
    communication style, 61
    community style, 77
    creative style, 65
    Jupiter and, 18, 44–45, 106–107, 115, 156, 219
    Moon and, 156–157
    Mutable modality, 18, 44–45, 59, 106
    Rising sign, 106–107
    Sun and, 44–45
    symbol, 18
Saturn
    Aquarius and, 48–49, 110–111, 115
    Capricorn and, 18, 46–47, 108–109, 115
    speed, 116
    symbol, 19
    transit speed, 116
Scorpio
    2nd House and, 208–209
    6th House and, 210
    10th House and, 211–212, 219
    balance calibration, 228

Scorpio, *continued*
   communication style, 61
   community style, 77
   creative style, 65
   Fixed modality, 18, 42–43, 105
   Mars and, 42–43, 104–105, 115,
      154, 210
   Moon and, 154–155
   Pluto and, 18, 42–43, 116, 154–155
   Rising sign, 104–105, 219
   Sun and, 42–43
   symbol, 18
Sun
   1st House and, 56–57
   2nd House and, 58–59
   3rd House and, 60–61
   4th House and, 62–63
   5th House and, 64–65, 228, 230
   6th House and, 66–67
   7th House and, 68–69, 118
   8th House and, 70–71
   9th House and, 72–73, 81
   10th House and, 74–75, 181
   11th House and, 76–77
   12th House and, 78–79
   Air element and, 25, 32–33
   Aquarius and, 48–49
   Aries and, 28–29
   calibration and, 231
   Cancer and, 34–35, 58
   Capricorn and, 46–47
   Gemini and, 32–33
   houses, 133
   Leo and, 18, 36–37, 56, 98–99, 115
   Libra and, 40–41, 60
   Pisces and, 50–51, 60
   Sagittarius and, 44–45
   Scorpio and, 42–43
   symbol, 19
   Taurus and, 30–31
   Virgo and, 38–39
symbols. *See individual planets;*
   zodiacal signs

T
Taurus
   2nd House and, 194
   6th House and, 66, 195–196

10th House and, 197, 205
12th House, 78
   balance calibration, 228
   communication style, 61
   community style, 77
   creative style, 65
   Fixed modality, 18, 30–31, 92,
      93, 194
   Moon and, 142–143
   Rising sign, 92–93
   ruled by Venus, 115
   ruling planet, 18, 30–31
   Sun and, 30–31
   symbol, 18
   Venus and, 18, 30–31, 92–93,
      115, 194, 197

U
Uranus
   1st House and, 198
   10th House and, 198
   Aquarius and, 18, 48–49, 116,
      160, 202
   Capricorn and, 158
   speed, 116
   symbol, 19
   transit speed, 116

V
Venus
   Libra and, 18, 40–41, 102–103,
      115, 152, 153, 201, 203, 205
   Scorpio and, 42–43
   speed, 116
   symbol, 19
   Taurus and, 18, 30–31, 92–93,
      115, 194, 197
   transit speed, 116
Virgo
   2nd House and, 194–195
   6th House and, 66, 196–197
   10th House and, 177, 198, 204
   balance calibration, 228
   communication style, 61
   community style, 77
   creative style, 65
   Mercury and, 38–39, 100–101,
      115, 118, 144, 150, 194

Moon and, 150–151
   Mutable modality, 18, 38–39,
      59, 100
   Rising sign, 100–101, 204
   Sun and, 38–39
   symbol, 18

W
Water element
   2nd House and, 208–209
   6th House and, 209–210
   10th House and, 211–212
   balance calibration, 227
   Cancer, 18, 34–35, 208,
      209–210, 211
   description of, 25
   Houses of Substance and, 187,
      188, 207–212
   inquiry approach, 73
   Pisces and, 18, 50–51, 209, 210,
      212
   Rising sign, 87
   Scorpio and, 18, 42–43, 208–209,
      210, 211–212
   Sun and, 25
Weight calibration, 224–225
Whole Sign Houses, 14, 16, 20,
   187, 190

Z
zodiacal signs. *See individual signs*